Rising from the Ashes into Church Renewal

Rising from the Ashes into Church Renewal

DESMOND BARRETT
Foreword by Ryan Giffin

WIPF & STOCK · Eugene, Oregon

RISING FROM THE ASHES INTO CHURCH RENEWAL

Copyright © 2025 Desmond Barrett. All rights reserved. Except for brief quotations in critical publications or reviews, no part of this book may be reproduced in any manner without prior written permission from the publisher. Write: Permissions, Wipf and Stock Publishers, 199 W. 8th Ave., Suite 3, Eugene, OR 97401.

Wipf & Stock
An Imprint of Wipf and Stock Publishers
199 W. 8th Ave., Suite 3
Eugene, OR 97401

www.wipfandstock.com

PAPERBACK ISBN: 979-8-3852-4273-3
HARDCOVER ISBN: 979-8-3852-4274-0
EBOOK ISBN: 979-8-3852-4275-7

03/13/25

THE HOLY BIBLE, NEW INTERNATIONAL VERSION®, NIV® Copyright © 1973, 1978, 1984, 2011 by Biblica, Inc.® Used by permission. All rights reserved worldwide.

To the faithful remnant of believers at Winter Haven Nazarene who refused to give up, walk away, or push back against the change when times got tough. Who continually prayed, sought God's guidance, obeyed his commands in the most challenging season in the church's life, and lived out the words "Believe Again," not as a campaign slogan but as a spiritual one. You have humbled me with your perseverance.

To the Church Board who stayed the course, sought God's will for the local church, found blessing in fellowship, and stayed united through it all. I could not have led without each of you walking beside me during this season. I will always be eternally grateful for what we have accomplished together.

Contents

Foreword by Ryan Giffin — ix

Introduction — xiii

Chapter 1: How Did It Get So Bad? — 1

Chapter 2: Rebuilding After Decline — 15

Chapter 3: Using Prayer to Focus the Church — 27

Chapter 4: Do the Work Today for Success Tomorrow — 37

Chapter 5: A Five-Year Cycle to Church Revitalization — 56

Chapter 6: Dreaming Through the Difficulty — 69

Chapter 7: Future-Forward Budgeting — 83

Chapter 8: Win One for Jesus — 98

Chapter 9: Believe Again: Dreaming Forward — 108

Chapter 10: The End Was Just the Beginning — 118

Epilogue: When God's Call Became My Yes — 122

Other Books by the Author — 125

Bibliography — 127

Foreword

JUST ABOUT ONCE A week, our office at Nazarene Archives receives an inquiry from a local church that is coming up on their centennial. These churches want to honor the milestone rightly, so they reach out to us for any information we may have on their history. We are glad to receive these calls. A milestone like that is certainly worth celebrating.

Churches do not turn one hundred years old—or even twenty years old—by accident. They do so because of the Holy Spirit's work through the wisdom and resolve of effective ministers and faithful laypeople throughout every era of the church's existence. The long-tenured pastors and the patriarchs and matriarchs of these congregations have seen them at their best and at their worst. These saints have endured and embraced change. They've given sacrificially. They've taken on ministries in the church that were beyond their comfort zone. They've participated in making tough decisions. They've supported leadership when it may not have been easy. They've kept showing up. They've worshipped. They've prayed. They've forgiven. And the witness of the church in their community continues to this day due in no small measure to the faithfulness of these local church heroes.

The globe is scattered with these kinds of "legacy churches," to use Dr. Desmond Barrett's helpful phrase. I first met Desmond at a missional training event both of us were participating in. One of the things I immediately appreciated about him was his sense of humor. He often had the whole room laughing. I imagine this gift of bringing levity has been a tremendous asset to the people and churches he has served. A church that prays together stays together, and a church that can laugh together can usually persist together.

Desmond knows this, and he knows a lot of other things about how to lead. A few years after our training, while I was pastoring the good people of Village Community Church in Kansas City, I was in search of a book our pastoral team could read together to help us through a season of revitalization. Desmond had recently written his book *Addition Through Subtraction: Revitalizing the Established Church*.[1] After perusing it, I knew it was exactly what we needed. It was filled with the kind of practical, immediately applicable wisdom that could inspire our team to both dream and act as we led our church. Furthermore, it was written by an author who truly loves the local church and wants to see her thrive. We ordered copies for the team, read a couple of chapters at a time, then gathered around a table for a meal and discussed what we were learning. We were better for it.

In the book you are currently holding in your hands, Desmond brings his love for the local church and his leadership elixir specifically to bear on churches with several years under their belt. Desmond currently pastors such a church, Winter Haven First Church of the Nazarene in Winter Haven, Florida. In this book you'll hear some of the stories of Winter Haven First and its ninety-three-year history. You'll read about Pastor Viva Crawford, the woman who planted the church in 1931 with an unquenching thirst to see residents of Winter Haven come to faith in Jesus Christ. You'll read about Pastor Don Newell and his inspiring vision to claim a whole city block for God's work. These are great stories, and wise pastors and church members will not underestimate their value as they steward the present moment in the life of their church. There are, however, other stories in this book—including several from Pastor Desmond's own recent history with Winter Haven First. As you read, you'll encounter the real-life challenges that come to good churches like these, and you'll also be given practical and godly wisdom for how those challenges can be met.

1. Barrett, *Addition Through Subtraction*.

Foreword

You'll feel like you are in conversation with a friend, and you'll feel encouraged, supported, and equipped as the Spirit uses you to help your church rise from the ashes into renewal. Read this book prayerfully, with a heart and mind wide open to what God may be asking of you and with a renewed sense of hope that the best days of your local church are ahead.

Dr. Ryan Giffin
Manager of the Church of the Nazarene Archives

Introduction

It was the first week at my new church. While sitting at my desk, working on a future sermon, the buildings and grounds committee chairperson walked into my office and handed me what I thought was a budget for the church. In reality it was seven hundred and seventy-one thousand dollars worth of deferred maintenance items that needed to be addressed on the church property. Unsurprisingly to me, the facility required work. A subcommittee of the church board who met me during the interview weekend was transparent and detailed needs of the facility. Still, the extent of the revelation was hundreds of thousands of dollars more than expected.

One week into my new assignment, I was overwhelmed with problems and needed more solutions to extract myself from the negative abyss of church business. The burden of the issues had weighed on this godly man who served as chair for several years, and in passing the paper to me, it was as if he was lifting the burden from his shoulders and placing it on mine. Afterward we spoke briefly about the list and the priorities he thought I should address first. As he walked out, I sat there motionless for a few minutes, contemplating my next steps. I had moved from a growing young church in another state to take on this challenge, a church that had an aging population and infrastructure, and all eyes were on me to turn around a ninety-three-year-old church, yet I had no plan.

Confused and worried about the prospects of the cause, I put my hands on my head, bowed it, and said, "Oh God, what have I done? Why did you call me here?" I dwelled only a bit on the negative and began focusing on developing a plan to carry us forward. The months ahead would be challenging and rewarding. Some would push me to sell the property and relocate the church; others would cheer on my service to renew the property and people. Through it all, a spiritual battle ensued for the church's soul, and it was not clear if the evil one would win, the church would fail and close, or if God would win out. Come what may, I was determined to fight to save a nearly one-hundred-year-old church from closing its doors and to begin to believe again in themselves, the community, and above all God.

In the coming pages is a story of great highs, deep valleys, fractures in relationships, fresh vision, and renewal as a legacy church fought to stay alive. The one question I asked myself countless times during the journey, which you should ask yourself if you serve in a legacy church as a pastor or church member: Will I give up before I start or choose to fight?

I decided to stay and fight. Will you?

Dr. Desmond Barrett

Chapter 1

How Did It Get So Bad?

THE CHURCH DID NOT start off wanting to decline. To be honest I do not think any church planter ever thought the church they would pour their heart and soul into would close. So, what happened? It was a question I asked walking into my new assignment. There is a stigma that an aging congregation is a dying congregation. If you were to ask any pastor if they want to go to an aging church and buildings with a host of deferred maintenance, many will run in the other direction. Who would blame them? However, there are pastors who feel the call to serve the comeback church and who see hope in decline. Countless pastors before and since have asked, Is God done with the local church that has seen better days? If not, are you being called to a church that is seen as hopeless, but God sees as hope filled? If you are a pastor or layperson in the church, the legacy church needs you. It needs your wisdom, and support.

In the first month of shepherding my new flock, I received the church historical records regarding attendance, membership, and financial giving. The records showed that the church had declined 60.04 percent in worship attendance in the last ten years. For thirteen straight years, there was a 66 percent decline in giving. But overall membership had stayed the same, letting me know that the membership rolls needed to be cleaned up. While I was not here to be a part of the decline, I was here now and could either blame others or find a way forward. While I could have complained about nearly one million dollars' worth of deferred maintenance, what good would it have done? I was humanly stuck and spiritually called by God to serve. There is no doubt that the pastors and the lay leadership before me did their best, patching the holes exposed by decline. Instead of seeing fault, my heart went out to them. Instead of fearing the numbers, I embraced them. God called me to serve during a season of decision in the life of the local church, decisions we would have to make to survive.

The Hartford Institute for Religion Research shared in their study, Exploring the Pandemic Impact on Congregations study, updated in 2023, that as "evident among Mainline Protestant churches, . . . nearly 50% of the average congregation is now over 65 years of age."[1] In the last three years, the decline of younger people has been dramatic. "The percentage of attendees under the age of 35 (all children, youth, and young adults) decreased from 37% in 2020, to 35% in 2021, and to 32% in 2023."[2] At this rate, the average church will have less than 25 percent under the age of thirty-five within the decade. So, if your local church has not aged, don't worry, it is coming. My church was in the latter category: an aging population, a building that had a lot of deferred maintenance, and a community that did not know we still existed. Many times early on I thought, could God have given me a bigger challenge?

REBOUND BY EMBRACING THE PEOPLE

As I reviewed the church grounds and financial situation in those early days, several staff members and a board member suggested rather frequently in the first month that we should sell the property and downsize the church. While it was tempting and maybe the easiest thing to do, I remembered the church's legacy—those

---

1. Hartford Institute for Religion Research, *Back to Normal*, 6.
2. Hartford Institute for Religion Research, *Back to Normal*, 6.

who had sowed into the building campaign to purchase the land and then build the buildings. I remembered the lives saved and given over at the altars. As a revitalization strategist, you must help the people remember that your role is to build from the past, not discredit it. I looked at the people who stayed throughout the decades of decline and felt I had to try. If not for God at least for the remaining people. The fact of the matter was the church voted just a year and half before I arrived to sell a large parcel next to the church, which housed Sunday school classes, church offices, a thrift store that the church ran, and parking lots, to get out of debt. If the church members did not want to sell everything then, why now? Nothing had changed except a new pastor. Maybe these "sellers" thought I was naïve, but this was not my first revitalization church, and I was not about to make a big mistake like announcing that we should sell the church and relocate at best, and at worst close the doors for good. With enormous pressure from raised expectations, trying was all anyone could do. Trying did not mean we would be successful, but it would mean we would give it our all. Deep down I felt God did not call me to help close the church but to help the church move from near death and into new life. The question that everyone was asking, and I was debating with God, was, Is the church worth saving?

In reading early on about the ninety-two-year history of the church at that time, the short answer was yes; the long answer was that we must recommit to God, the land, and the neighborhood in which we were planted if we would rebound. Recommitting is essential for any legacy church to have new life, saying to yourself and to the community that the church does not give up on God or the community. A two-word anthem rang forth in those early days: "Believe again!" The people who made up the church had to believe again that God could use them, us, to reach out to the community. The fact is that hard choices had to be made, starting with reclaiming the property for the Lord. It was not the first time the church leadership had to commit to the property. In the mid-1950s, Pastor Don Newell, who would serve for nearly eleven years, envisioned claiming a whole city block for God's work. This was a God moment for a church running less than sixty weekly attenders on just an acre of land. The story goes that Pastor Newell was preparing his sermon in his pastoral study when he felt prompted by the Holy Spirit to stop what he was doing and exit his office. In obedience he stopped and went out onto the sidewalk in front of the church. Looking around, he felt again prompted by the Spirit to walk to the stop sign. As he stopped, he felt the Lord lead him to claim the land he had just walked for future ministries. He would be prompted several more times until he walked the whole city block, claiming the land for Jesus. The block he had encircled with prayers was disjointed land: a mix of city and private property, residential lots, and limited commercial buildings making up the city block. God gave Pastor Newell a dream to claim the land for future expansion of the kingdom. While Pastor Newell would never see the land entirely in the church's name, God answered the promise in 2008—four years into its unknown decline. In a miracle, the last piece of the city block was bought, thus completing God's plan, fifty years after the proclamation. Think about this: If God could put together pieces of property fifty-plus years on, what could he do now in your church or life? See it this way, God has a plan, but will you trust him? Will the church trust him to fulfill all his promises?

After learning the story in my first month, God spoke to my spirit and clearly said, "Do not sell." Even after nearly two decades of decline, to sell now was not a choice for me and others, soon enough, because we realized God had a plan, and it started now. We (his church) had to recommit to his plan. Each person who made up the church was just one small piece in a more significant kingdom move in our city. If the staff would not back the renewal plan God was providing, I prayed that the church board would and the people in the pew would follow suit. If your church wants to find its blessing, it must fully submit to God's will and then recommit to his plan for the church. As for me, I was fully committed to his plan for the church.

Rebound by Reconnecting

When leading a church through decline and back into vibrancy, there is a tendency to lash out at others. First, at the community for not engaging the local church through visits. Secondly, at members who left the church and gave up on God and the people who remained as the downturn deepened. Third, the pastors or lay leadership who led during a season of decline because they should have done something. Be honest: What is the use? Another way to look at it is, Why go back in time to rehash the negative story of the past, unless you want to learn from it? Blaming someone or a situation is not the right answer. It will not change the facts or the circumstances in which the church finds itself today. So instead of complaining about the past, begin to rebound from the past by reconnecting with God through prayer, small groups focusing on reaching new people, and engaging people right where you meet them. Throughout Scripture, leaders who faced opposition were seen praying. Why? Because prayer unlocks the power of God to unleash his influence upon the church. In other words, prayer power activates the spiritual hearts of the people and reconnects the church to the word of God. Ask yourself and the church board: Do you want the church to grow? Then pray. Do you want new members? Then pray. Do you want to reach your community? Then pray. Quit looking for a silver bullet and PRAY!

As the church activates God's power through prayer, it becomes open to his desires for the local church. Through prayer, the remaining people must relinquish personal desires for God's will. The hardest part of reconnecting to God, to each other, and the community is letting go. I get it that when things were bad you had to huddle together to save the church. But God wants to move you from a holy-huddle church to an arms-stretched-wide church seeking community partners. God used the small remnant of believers to keep his church going strong, and so too for the aging church. While the world may decry growing older, you should rejoice in the faithful congregation God has given you to be a part of. The rest of your church's stories, like ours, are yet to be written.

I want to encourage you early on in this resource that God is not done with the legacy church, and better days are ahead.

CHASING THE PAST

Every church that has been open more than a few years has set in motion the way "things have always been done." The leadership team sets down markers for growth, spiritual renewal, programs, partnerships, and precedents each year. Many of these are unintended and only come about because they fit the current reality that the church is facing. For many leaders and members, it freezes what should or should not be done from then on. "This is how we have always done it" sneaks up on churches and becomes set in stone overnight. The reality is that these innocent activities have set down small idols for some at the church, and to break from "tradition" is almost anti-religious. The past is symbolized by refusing to move things from their current position, changing the decor, or even removing a piece of furniture in fear of losing memories. The mindset of the past holds captive churches and leaders who want to move forward but are unable or even unwilling to do so out of fear of hurting someone.

The Past Is the Hero

A legacy church has a rich history of tremendous highs and incredible lows. Looking back on the history, you can see the moments where God moved; in those seasons, the marker of "hero" is set in place. The shadow of that pastoral leader, who led the time of the great awakening of growth through numerical increase, new buildings, campus relocation, or large community gatherings, begins to loom large over the latter leaders to come. Those "glory days" are held in high esteem by members who were there during the exciting years of development. As the paradigm has shifted to slower growth or even decline, the need for a leader-savior in some people's mind becomes more vital as the emotions of what was and what has come is put into focus.

If you are serving in a church that is "hero-worshiping" the past, begin to help them see that the past cannot dictate the future but can help the church know the potential of the church. Honoring former leaders and the church's history celebrates what God did but is a reminder of what God can do again. God is doing a new work inside of the church, and while the past is remarkable, God has plans that fit your current neighborhood and where he hopes to lead your congregation. Begin by helping your church focus on the main thing, Jesus, not people, and watch how things begin to happen earnestly.

The Past Dictates the Future

In whatever assignment God has placed me, I have had to deal with the past as I have tried to help the church enter the new God chapter, realizing that the past is not the enemy nor the people who harken back to the days when everything was great in their eyes. Recently, I had a conversation with a lay member who was putting together the communion elements. I asked a simple, thought-provoking question: Why do we as a church place a cloth over the communion elements? The dear sister said, "I don't know. That was how I had been taught." Her answer was honest and revealing.

Some may say the cloth represents the faithfulness of Christ, a reminder of Christ's funeral garments, or even to keep flies off the elements before the advent of air conditioning. But for me this one example showed how when a pattern sets in, it traps exploring different ways of doing things. My dedicated volunteer was doing everything correctly; the volunteer was doing it all right. She was doing what the previous volunteer taught her. Now take the situation I shared back to your current church. What needs to be talked through more clearly? What if the church you're serving is in yesteryear but living in today? What if your church is missing out on what God is doing now because the church is so focused on yesterday? Let me encourage you, refrain from falling into the pattern of doing something that looks right but feels wrong. Begin to lead your people to pray for what God wants them to do right now. Become a "right now" serving church that reaches the needs of those inside and outside the church. Begin to pray and allow the Spirit to guide you to the plan that God has. Then enable the future to dictate your pattern of serving, one step of obedience at a time.

The glory days are not behind your local church but before them. There are people right now in the community where you serve that need your people, programs, and love for the community. Be a church where people feel welcome to enter and find a home in the pews. God has a perfect plan for your church if you are willing to chase the present more than the past.

DO NOT IGNORE THE PAST

Throughout the latter half of the last decade, a spiritual wind has refocused church leadership to reevaluate the legacy church or, as some call it, the established church. The fact of the matter is that most denominations are declining. One of the largest denominations, the Southern Baptist Convention, reports that "among the 50,423 active congregations in the Southern Baptist Convention in 2021, 2% disbanded or closed and 0.5% left or were disaffiliated from the Convention by the time the 2022 data was compiled."[3] Most churches are stagnant or dying. Revitalization will not be an offshoot of the church growth movement but a new mainstay in redeveloping the local church to reach the community in new ways.

More and more pastors and congregations will have to come to the reality that revitalization must become a vital part of church health. The idea that churches will keep growing if they just provide good music, strong preaching, and active programming is outdated. For your church to be revitalized, it will need clear direction, fresh community insight, redeeming values that will connect the church with future generations, and expanded community connections that gather in and outside the local church. The work

---

3. Earls, "Southern Baptists."

that needs to be done will be built on the strong foundation of the past and cannot be discarded or started over. The work the legacy church has accomplished should be celebrated and applauded, but it cannot be frozen in time.

Legacy Churches Need Vision, Leadership, and Clear Direction

Studies have shown that most evangelical churches in North America are in some state of decline. Even my own denomination (Church of the Nazarene) has seen a significant decline of "-11.56% in the USA/Canada Region" in the past decade while other regions around the world have seen steady growth.[4] With decreasing membership, aging buildings, deferred maintenance, and lack of community engagement, the legacy church has seen its numbers reduce. While some outlier churches have seen an increase in attendance and community engagement, most are facing a crisis moment to either reengage or close the local church. I want you to pause and reflect on your own local church. Does this speak of what you are facing? If so, know your local church is not alone. It is happening all across the board regardless of denominational affiliation.

In the past the concept of a church hiring a younger pastor as the silver bullet became a misguided spiritual pipe dream. The sad truth is that there are not enough younger pastors in the pipeline to fill all the pulpits needed in the next ten years. Baby Boomers (those born 1946–1964) continue to retire, and the early wave of Generation X (those born 1965–1980) begins to leave the pulpits for retirement. The local church has entered a warning zone. "Data collected by the Association of Theological Schools shows that the number of students enrolled in master of divinity degrees—required for ordination in many mainline denominations—is down 9% since 2018."[5] Who will replace these leaders if denominations do not have trained clergy in the ministry pipeline?

---

4. Nazarene News Staff, "General Secretary."
5. Evans, "Redefining Ministry."

The legacy church needs visionary pastors who see what could be, not where the local church finds itself today. The revitalizer's role is to help the church see the need and lead it into a new future defined not by programs but by the needs of people in the shadow of the steeple. The revitalizer will need to help the church reengage the community, embrace community needs, and overlay those needs in a spiritual context that embraces the marketplace. This role is exciting yet challenging and will need a person with a clear vision and discernable leadership qualities that will help the legacy church to become a church back on a mission.

Legacy Churches Need a Fresh Perceptive to Reach the Community Around Them

As you drive throughout your community, begin to see the picture of who the community is and where it needs to go. Slow down and view the community with Jesus' eyes. By evaluating the needs around you, you can better understand the community culture and the complex nature of returning the church to the streets to meet its neighbors. For many older members in the established church, everything around them has changed except the church. Their family has grown up and moved away. Friends have passed away or no longer attend because of health reasons. Yet each Sunday the church is the same. Realize that any change brought to the church might be met with pushback from those members holding on to the last vestiges of the past. Revitalization pushback is not against you but the passage of time.

In the last decade, 123 members had passed and entered glory. One hundred and twenty-three active members left a hole in the local church's life. As some passed away, family members donated funds to purchase furniture or funds for a significant project. As a token of appreciation, the church honored their love with a little gold plaque recognizing their accomplishment and love of the local church.

Plaques or other recognitions become small idols in the local church, and instead of honoring someone, they become their tombstone of remembrance. Over time, these plaques become far more important than repositioning the church to reach new people; thus, no new people come, or at least stay, but the plaques do. Hear my heart: I am not against recognizing or honoring someone in the church. However, if the honor becomes more important than winning souls, it will overshadow the original call of service in the local church.

A church revitalizer enters the church community understanding that they are called not to deconstruct the local church but to reconstruct the hopes and dreams of those members still sitting in the pew. Through observation, conversations, and relationships, the revitalizer guides the church into a new season in the church's life by listening to members' fears and encouraging their faith. Leaning into these stories, gather stories of where God was and is at work and help the people recapture the God dreams they have for the local church.

Through a fresh outlook ladened with positive antidotes and encouraging celebrations highlighting small and large wins, the revitalizer can provide new opportunities for the church and community to connect. Dream about what could be leveraging the church campus with the community needs.

Legacy Churches Have Incredible Legacies That Need Redeeming for This Generation

When a revitalizer comes to a church for the first time, they must realize that God has worked inside the church for decades. Realize that changing something out of hand might be so destructive that it terminates the ministry before it really begins, so do not go in too fast. Instead, the church revitalizer should become the church's leading historian, understanding the past to reengage the past with the present. The history of a local church is not to be buried but honored. Think for a moment: Why are all the nameplates and plaques around a church? It is about celebrating the heroes of the church who strived to serve God and the local church faithfully over the decades. Honoring the past should be done in a way that captures the moment the church is living in. One of the ways of honoring the past is developing a legacy wall or living museum in your lobby where you can share the past through pictures, awards, and stories. It connects the past to the future and enables the continuance of God's move in the church.

Every church you have been a part of was started by amazing God-called people, who had a heart for the neighborhood where the church was planted. That legacy must not be lost to history as you begin to revitalize the church. Instead of throwing out the past, begin to honor it through a Legacy Wall—a wall that captures and highlights the storied history of the church throughout the decades. As we remade the lobby, we ensured a large eight-foot by nine-foot area became our legacy wall. On the wall is the story of our church told through pictures of pastors and buildings, along with biographies of accomplishments or challenges under each pastor. In front of the wall, clear cases on pedals highlight important artifacts from the past, and a two-sided divider is curated quarterly to highlight a theme from the past, such as church birthdays, Sunday school accomplishments, etc., which continue to carry forward the story of yesterday with today. Instead of seeing the lobby as a mausoleum to the past, see it as an opportunity to celebrate and educate the current and future members on the history of the church.

Mark Clifton, the senior director of replanting at the North American Mission Board for the Southern Baptist Convention, said, "My passion for replanting came when God brought one thought to my mind, and that was this: 'What about a dying church brings glory to God? What about a dying church says our God is great and His Gospel is powerful?' And then I realized that trying to reclaim dying churches was not primarily a mission endeavor, or an endeavor to help the Convention (SBC). It was an endeavor to reclaim God's glory. So, it's really an act of worship."[6] Redeeming the legacy church is not for a pastor, church board, or the person in the pew. It is to honor God through renewed faithfulness to build and expand the community. As a leader, celebrate the past,

---

6. Chandler, "Mark Clifton."

How Did It Get So Bad?

evaluate the present, and prepare for the future. That may mean some plaques and nameplates are relocated to the legacy wall as the church redesigns former offices into classrooms and pews into chairs. Hear my heart on this: relocating the honorary nameplates does not remove the honor but extends the legacy as the church continues reconfiguring the space to reach new people with the gospel.

Legacy Churches Have Resources That God Can Use to Expand Kingdom Connections

What the local church might lack in church membership it makes up for in resources (buildings, financial accounts, and the overall property). As a church leadership team, you must begin to see these resources as something other than tangible or even transactional, but as a tool to do effective ministry. The leader helps the remaining church members recapture the community's vision by leveraging the resources they currently have to engage the community in new ways. That may mean remapping (relocating classes or transforming space into something new) the campus and the ministries housed in certain rooms in the building; relocating them to new areas with a design for future connections; or what about using some of the financial resources to tackle deferred maintenance issues by updating high-traffic areas for future guests' enjoyment (lobby, parking lot, or restrooms). How about viewing the church property not as a gathering place for members but as a future gathering space for community events in partnership with area service clubs or nonprofit social agencies. Whatever you can dream, God can provide.

For instance, that might look like moving parking bumpers from one of your parking lots to open the space for a future community playground, or tearing down an old shed to provide space for a new picnic shelter for the community to use. Remember, revitalizer, there is no silver bullet to reach the community, but little by little change will come. Each project contextualized to fit the local church and community needs can recapture the imagination of the church-community relationship. At the end of the day, the goal should be to leverage the church's resources to help the community while helping the church become a more gospel-centered witness in the community it was planted in decades ago.

Chapter 2

Rebuilding After Decline

FOR THE LAST SEVERAL years, churches have allowed the pandemic (or put in your major problem) to be the "bogeyman" of the church. Leaders have named it, claimed it, and discussed it as the significant effect of decline within the local church. However, there comes a time when the church must move from the negative feelings of leading a church in decline to focusing on rebuilding. Rebuilding after a pandemic, moral failure, neighborhood decline, etc., is difficult. For the longest time, decline was seen as the pastor's fault, but today it should be seen as a microcosm of a significant societal shift. Instead of ignoring the decline, the church has an opportunity to look at ways to rebuild from the loss. For decades, everything our church did turned to gold. There was no stopping the church from growing to nearly six hundred people. But as the neighborhood around the church changed, the church got left behind. The once-thriving downtown corridor became a ghost town of shuttered businesses, the homes around the church became transient at best, and many members began to drift away. What was left? Aging buildings and people—a mighty remnant of what was but what could be again.

From the outside, the paint on the buildings had faded, old signage bleached by the hot tropical sun, and a spirit of resignation set in. But God had another plan. As developers began reshaping downtown, they had an eye on the two city blocks the church owed. Through many hard conversations, a deal was struck to release us from debt and sow seeds for a new neighborhood by selling one city block. Even then, others felt we should sell everything and move away from the city center. Others were left angered over the sale of the property in the first place and walked away. Two local churches wanted the remainder of the church's property, one swapping church buildings with the other through a sale. But God wanted us to stay and fight. And fight we have. God had not given up on his church, and we had not given up on him.

Evaluate Where the Church Finds Itself

Instead of seeing decline as a negative, a rebuilding leader sees it as an opportunity to reimagine the local church into a missional enterprise, not just a Sunday morning attractional model. Believe me, when you find yourself in a church decline, there are a lot of people to blame. But placing faith in each other and God, the rebuilding leader invites members to discuss openly where they feel the church should go. It should not be a negative session where one member disparages another, but a time of true reflection on where the church has been, is now, and where it can go well into the future. Let the words of Pastor Ryan Burge, the former pastor of First Baptist Church of Mount Vernon, Illinois, be a warning to your own thinking and work: "After a couple of years, the discussion about revitalizing the church began to grow quiet. A sense of resignation started to creep in. I came to a disheartening conclusion: I wasn't going to be able to turn things around. I think at that point most members knew in their hearts that the end was coming for the church. We were just all afraid to speak that truth into existence. It was better to keep our heads down and focus on the next worship service and not worry about what would happen in three or five years."[1]

---

1. Burge, "My Church Is Closing."

In the evaluation stage, focus on the church's spiritual health, what keeps current members, what is stopping the retention of visitors, what the communities' needs are, and how the church can partner. This process is slow but should be deliberate in finding a new way forward. A rebuilding leader understands that sometimes a little prodding can help the mission.

Elevate the Programs and People That Are Helping the Church Move Forward

In every church, there is always something that can be celebrated when reviewing the workings of the local church. As a rebuilder you must find it, praise it, and relay where God works. Even if there is pushback. Stay positive, for your work is not easy but desperately needed, even if the church does not realize it just yet. As you evaluate programs, positions, etc., some will need to be retired, and others need to be elevated to a new level. Help the church see the positive aspects of programs and people that you currently have by reviewing your church leadership items that may have been left unaddressed in the past. Reimagine the space (square footage and acreage the church sits on) and its uses while seeking a new way forward. Help the church rethink how programs impact inside and outside. Use the church's decline to the church's advantage to become nimbler in making decisions.

I am excited, and you should be too, that God has a great plan for your local church. Let me challenge you to pray. It will take prayers and a dedicated capacity to see what others do not see to help the church rebound.

Experiment with Ideas and Programs That Might Have Felt Risky in the Past

Think of the decline not as a negative but an exciting opportunity to rebirth the local church. When your local church was built, it was the right church for the community it was born into. It might not have adapted to the community's changing neighborhood or cultural norms, but it stayed open. Instead of ebbing with the community's needs, many churches circled the spiritual wagons and hoped the outside world would not intrude on what they were trying to accomplish. It left the church unprepared for what was to come. But what an opportunity to rebound by rebranding how the church interacts with the community.

Experiment with ideas and programs that might have challenged the church's footprint in the past, and see what sticks. Far too many churches have a fear and faith problem, which has frozen them in a state of decline. Help the church move past fear into a new spiritual awakening of their faith and try something. Think creatively. Think strategically using the assets you have to minister to the people you want to reach. "The result is that congregations are closing and merging with others, leaving some capacious sanctuaries and outlying buildings underused or unused altogether. Many religious organizations are having to rethink how to make the best use of their largest assets—the building as well as the underlying land—and give them a second life."[2] If the church is to live again, it must find new creative ways to leverage the church resources to build relationships with the neighborhood and community at large.

In 1982, under Pastor Charles Kirby, the church built the first of two sanctuaries, each more magnificent than the former. By 1988, the church had grown so large that a twelve hundred-person sanctuary was built, and the "old" 1982 sanctuary would become the gym. Over the next several decades, as the church began to decline, the gym was used less and less. When I arrived, it was used for our homeless ministry services weekly and Upward Basketball each spring. But it mainly sat empty, waiting to reclaim its former glory.

The sanctuary beams had become black with mold, the former baptismal area had nearly three feet of black mold marching down its walls, and the gym floor had outlived its lifespan. I saw a community connection opportunity through the black mold and

2. Rosen, "Hotel and Restaurants."

lack of full ministry opportunities that could happen in the space, but several things would have to take place. In time, redemption would come to this space. We would recapture this space for a future community center. The struggles to come would be real and are covered elsewhere in this book. But know this truth: if you can dream, God can fulfill it if it's his dream in the first place.

Execute the Vision and Plan That God Has Placed on the Church's Heart

God has a plan for the local church, and he will use you to help resurrect the church. There is a tendency for rebuilders to start from scratch when they lead from a station of decline. Instead of starting over, begin where the church is. Build off of the church's legacy. Highlight past accomplishments. Celebrate what God has done and what he will do again. Spend some time praying, seeking God's will for the church. Listen with an attentive ear as you speak with current and former members of the church. Learn what worked in the past and what could work in the future. If you slow down and observe, the plan is right before you, in the people you serve. Allow God to lead and watch what happens.

As the plan comes to fruition, you might need to lay it out in phases, as one big thing might be too much of a change out of the gate. Instead, staggering the phases will help current members process the change and vision while creating momentum for the Lord's work to come. Understand that whatever the plan, implantation will take adaptability. Be an optimistic church leader, as the best days for the local church are bright. Be encouraged in rebuilding from decline by staying centered on the word, living out a missional vision, and finding creative ways to keep Jesus at the forefront of the local church's work.

DYING TO LIVE

In the season of desperation, a person will either hold on to the last vestiges of the church or cling to the garment of Christ's robe. In each scenario, that idea of dying compels a church to resist change or radically submit to change. The death scenario is playing out in every denomination and community around the United States. The idea that "it won't happen to my church" is a misconception that will find the church unprepared to live. Sometimes church members sit in the heyday of the church and miss the signs of decline all around them.

I met with a church member for nearly two and a half hours to discuss the church's financial picture as we began implementing the turnaround plan. Early in the conversation, he shared that he did not vote for me to become the church pastor during the recent pastoral search. He was one of fourteen people who voted no several months before. In my office, he wanted to share that his gut had been wrong and tried to encourage me and offer support, but he also raised a few questions. He saw the need for a worship pastor, which would enhance the Sunday morning gathering. He believed that the "Believe Again" plan, which was voted on and approved by the church board twice in the previous three months, was a facility-focused program and not a real outreach plan. He shared that I also needed to focus on the church by:

1. Good preaching and being a dynamic pastor.
2. Worship music led by a song leader, as we were known as a musically gifted church in the past.
3. Focus on youth and children, as there was only my son and two other children who came once or twice a month.

He was right on all counts. We would have been moving in the same direction if he had just stopped there. "If we build to two hundred attendees in our second service, we will solve our problems," he said. As I mentioned to him, we had to cut, or at least reorganize, the budget by eliminating areas of current staff/programs to implement his plan. He strongly disagreed. I tried to get across that pastors do not build churches, the people do by inviting one person at a time. He said, "A pastor, music, and strong youth/children's department will turn this church around." Well, he was right again; we disagreed on what would come next to accomplish our goals, but on the overall vision, we agreed.

Again, if he stopped there, we would be close to complete agreement. He then asked, "How long do you plan to stay?" Thinking on what was asked, I answered that in five years, I would be fifty years old and would evaluate my ministry and life at that time, if God had not released me before. He, in turn, said, "You are using this church as a stepping stone to another church." I smiled and said, "This church is no longer a stepping stone church, but it could be my tombstone if things don't turn around." Sitting in silence after that statement, I realized that even as we were dying, members like him did not see what needed to take place to move back into spiritual and physical growth as a church. God has a fantastic plan for the local church, but it seems people continue to block or distort his plan for their selfish emotions and personal preferences. If your local church is going to live, it will have to commit to a greater vision, commit to each other, and commit to an extraordinary God.

Commit to a Greater Vision

Over the years, as the church began to die, the vision for others became inward. The church leadership batted down proposed program and funds to host a new ministry because of an innate need of protecting the status quo. The leadership might argue with that assessment by me, but their actions spoke louder than words because I was living in their decades of results. Through a self-fulfilling prophecy, the church began to lack the funds and people they desired to reach with the gospel. Hebrews 12:1 reminds the reader that there is a "great cloud of witnesses," those of faith cheering the church on, yet the local church finds itself in a death spiral spinning out of control because it forgot to give the church over to God, who is in complete control.

Some revitalization strategists, and maybe even leaders in your denomination, believe legacy churches should die, and their funds should be reinvested in church planting. I am not one of them. Churches and denominations should invest in revitalizing churches so when healthy, the legacy churches can use their wealth of spiritual, physical, and financial knowledge to plant new, healthy churches. The local church has to commit to a greater vision that obeys God's will and begin to use church facilities and campus for significant community impact. Suppose your local church has a smaller footprint than before (fewer people). In that case, you will have more buildings (space in general) that are underutilized. Reimagine the space through partnerships with nonprofits, private schools, childcare facilities, homeschool groups, or meeting spaces.

There is an adage: if you build it, they will come. God will send new partners if the church can reimagine its current space with a gospel-centered community focus. Reversing a church's decline is more about positive biblical vision and direction than gimmicks. As change in our church began to happen, one member expressed her displeasure by saying, "Desmond, you would rent a piece of grass to get new revenue." No. But I would share unused space with a partner to share the cost of the facilities. It would enable the church to reinvest the revenue in the declining infrastructure while bringing people onto the property more than just on Sunday. A win-win in my book.

Commit to Each Other

As our legacy church declined, a mighty remnant of believers held to the calling of keeping the church doors open. What a blessing to reflect on the few that fought to keep our story alive. Most held fast to the promise of a better day to come. Others left during the turmoil that came with change. Can I caution you: if you find yourself in a church with just a handful of people, see it as an opportunity to commit to each other, to pray, and to encourage one another in your daily walk with the Lord. Know that some will leave, as the pain will be too much. As the church laid dormant and began to die, discouragement took hold and in turn forced the church to dig deeper to find encouragement with such discouraging news. In an ever-changing world, the legacy church has become a safe space for those who have lost so much. Stop and think about the challenges beyond just offering and maintaining a building. The people in the pews have aged with the slow decline of death. Their spouse has gone to heaven, the children they once brought to church grew up and moved away, and now, once-dear friends have either become too old to attend or have moved on to another church, disillusioned by what was left. Yet, safety is sitting in the same pew they have sat in for decades. The church may not be a building, but the church building offers so much comfort to its long-term members.

The incubator for new ideas to rebound from decline and to hope for new solutions to old problems, for future growth, is prayer. As the church moves forward, it must commit to praying earnestly for each other and the neighborhood. It is not one or the other but a multipronged approach to seeking after the will of God. In essence, prayer becomes the spiritual priming agent for the new well that will spring forth new life.

Commit to Foundational Views of Serving Others as Christ

When the church is slowly dying, there is a tendency to cut itself off from the ever-changing neighborhood around it. Instead of putting up barriers between the church and community, begin to see the community as a helpmate in redeeming the church. As Christ is in the church, so too he is in the neighborhood. Imagine how the church could open its campus as a community park with a new playground, a dog park in a fenced-in area, or put up a large picnic shelter where the neighborhood could host community yard sales or birthday parties. Begin to imagine the community and the church with eyes outward instead of eyes inward on the church's needs.

The community outside the church's walls needs a Bible-teaching church as much as the church needs a community that is invested in what it offers. God is in the redeeming business, and he wants to redeem the local church, but you must do your part in developing a community-centric focus on reaching the lost through the local church. The turnaround the church desires will not happen overnight, but through a commitment to serving others, Jesus' redemption will not be just a wish but a reality with time.

EXPLORING LOSS IN THE CHURCH

Loss of any kind is painful, but losing someone who used to be a cheerleader in the church is hurtful in so many ways. Even in loss you find a new way forward. Leading in any form alienates some and highlights others as the progress of change marches on. Even small changes bring about many issues that pastors and congregations deal with in a changing season. Every day, each hour, our hearts long to grow closer and closer to God as a leader, to feel his connection, love, and admiration. But life triggers us—pulls us away, really—to wish for what was, and what wasn't. The heart and mind battle for the soul, the spiritual tug-of-war, is real, and it leaves you hurt, lost, and broken. At the end of ourselves, it is there that we are ready for Christ. I have seen and experienced the pain when members left. They left during these early and middle stages of the turnaround. I felt the arrows thrown at me for changing the church. You don't get over the loss that comes with growth, but you do keep trusting God.

Grief in all its forms is cruel yet healing. The church can only capture God's promise attained through Jesus by dying to self. At times, emotion takes hold where compassion should have been shown; anger overtakes thinking where there should have been love. It is where logic overrules God's peace amid turmoil. Members in the church community may run from God, pointing fingers at your leadership abilities and preaching style, but know that it's not you, it's them. Healing can come, with his help; we can move forward sometimes together and other times separately.

My scars are numerous from revitalizing churches, but throughout each step of the process, I keep trusting the one who called me: God. The calling and work of revitalization is needed, so do not give up, just dig in with God.

So, what do you do when others leave? Transitions of any type (death, job, moving) bring forth the rawness of emotion that frightens and challenges individuals to the core, but just then you become open to growing deeper with Jesus. In the deepening, a church moves from a self-focused to a God-focused church. It is painful as Jesus removes pride, wants, and desires and restores His will in the local church. Through the pain of deepening, the progress of spiritual growth endures and reveals in its growth plan what is next. Through the processing of loss, the church begins to see new opportunities where God is leading.

Target Frustrations to Attain Fruit, Not Fault

Anyone can point out what is not working, but only a few are willing to point out mistakes and then provide two to three solutions to the problem. The church does not need any more negative talk, backstabbing, or innuendos; the world has given us enough of that. Pastors do not need to play spiritual chess with their congregation to manipulate their way forward; both need a God-honoring, God-called leadership team that follows God's call for the local church. God will honor requests as leaders begin to target frustrations (what is holding the church back) to attain fruit (which is spirit-filled members and spiritual health) by finding commonality in serving the local church.

I must caution you again: it is not going to be easy. It will take a tenacious, determined leader and church board not to give up when resistance to change occurs. Member and pastor must look for something other than fault in what is being said about them or their situation and seek to find the fruit. Even in the most negative comments, there are sometimes grains of truth. Challenge yourself to keep the truth and discard the rest. Begin to learn from the challenge you face at the present time, and allow it to grow you into a better member of the local church.

Seek a Way Forward from Loss

Fear is natural. Fear of the unknown is something most people have experienced. The church I found was fearful. The leaders were afraid we would die without a fight. Members feared the change mandate being asked of them. In every church there are black-and-white numbers found on the financial ledger, denominational reporting on baptisms, baby dedications, new members, deaths, etc., that do not lie. Members or leaders might lie to themselves about the decline, but these numbers are what they are. Loss of people, programs, or even positions can cause a momentary freezing for a church leader. As you begin to navigate through loss and come out the other side, allow God to be your guide. The church is entering a spiritual field that will take prayerful determination to overcome and come out victorious. The evil one wants nothing more than to destroy what God is doing inside your heart as a leader and in the church. See it more as a badge of honor that you keep getting pushback because it must mean you are on the God road. Keep pressing forward by staying positive, prayerful, and positioned to move when God tells you and the church to move.

As a leader, you must stay positive as you help explore the future of what God wants in the church. Positivity will overcome negativity in the end. In the short run it may look hopeless, but positivity will win the day with God. Keep pointing your people to prayer by seeking God daily yourself. Get the church in a position to advance into the new kingdom efforts, once the loss period has ended, by trusting God today.

Remember Jesus WINS in the end. As the church stays Christ-honoring, Christ's healing will come over each member. A time of renewal will come about as you target frustrations to attain fruit and a way forward from loss.

Chapter 3

Using Prayer to Focus the Church

THERE IS A TENDENCY to wonder, "What am I doing?" That feeling of spinning your wheels and not seeing any fruit from your preaching, teaching, and leading in the church. You might even scroll through social media and see the "successes" of other churches and ask again, "What am I doing?" Today's leaders live in a fishbowl watched on all sides by members and nonattenders. Many times, the expectation of those in the church is that numbers mean effectiveness. When effectiveness is measured differently by God.

I cannot picture God hanging over the banister of heaven looking down and counting people in pews or how many people gave this past week to the local church. I sense he is looking for a heart change rather than how much change is in the offering plate. God has a plan for each church and its leader. He has a plan that will surprise and delight your imagination if you stay faithful to the calling. The growth pastor who built up the church from sixty to nearly six hundred in ten years in the 1980s, Pastor Charles Kirby, was fond of saying, "God is never late; he is right on time," and it's a reminder that God's plan is never late.

God Is Calling the Church to Gather and Listen

Is there an easy way to lead the local church through the change it has experienced? If so, I have not found it, but when I stop, pray, and seek God's direction, I begin to pick up a sense of direction I did not have before. What happened? It was removing my power and plugging into God's power for the local church. Each week in reviewing the bulletin, you might get overwhelmed by all the service opportunities in the church and miss the real reason for service on Sunday. The busyness that has overtaken the world has now infiltrated the church and has kept many from focusing on God.

Busyness can lead to complacency, and complacency leads to decline. When a church spends time in dedicated prayer seeking the inspiration of God, they begin to turn the attention from self to the Savior. At that very moment, the church is open in order to listen to God and hear the direction in which he is moving. Gathering times do not necessarily have to be at a typical service time; it can be a special called prayer time. Focused prayer becomes God's gathering place to transform the church and break through into where he wants to lead.

God Is Calling the Church to Obey His Commands

As the church turns to prayer, the enemy will want nothing more than to defeat the church in the infancy of the new focus. Stay focused not on the enemy but on why the church has come together to pray. Prayer should be seen as the motor of the church, to focus the church on the commands. "It is written," Jesus said to the disciples, "My house will be called a house of prayer." (Matt 21:13). Turning prayer into a movement that captures the soul of the church recreates the day the church was birthed and the passion of serving God and the community.

Prayer essentially brings the holy fire down upon the church and its situation. The command of God to pray without ceasing (1 Thess 5:17) is one the church needs to practice daily, not just when things are tough around the church. God has a fantastic plan for the local church, but the church must believe and then lean into that plan by doing its part in calling the church to pray regularly for the community, the needs, and the requests of others.

God Is Calling the Church to Do Its Part in the Life of Others

Outside the four walls of the local church is a community that desperately needs its influence. The world radically approves of the nature of sin that the Bible speaks against. Think about the opportunity the church has to be at the forefront of conveying God's love, grace, and hope into the sin-filled world. Instead of hiding inside the four walls, the church can step out into the lives of those struggling in sin and lead them into the forgiving love of Christ. It will not be easy, but it will be seen as an act of compassion, as Christ was compassionate to you when he took you out of sin.

Look around the community and see where your local church can join in helping where God is already at work. Maybe it's a nonprofit that speaks to the church's heart. A single mother who needs extra yard work completed. Or an elderly member who needs repairs done to the home and meals brought in weekly. When you begin to pray with a focus for "eyes wide open" on others, God will reveal his plan for your local church. A willing church fully surrendered through a life of prayer captures the blessing of the church and, thus, the blessing of God in the act of loving on those in need in the community.

A church that prays is a church that changes its focus from self to the Savior and redeems the time for God's will in the church's life. Be faithful to the call, and guide your church to gather. Listen to what God is saying. Obey his commands, and serve as the light in a dark world. Weekly, I walk into the vast, empty sanctuary during the week and pray for God over the pews, which represent people, families, here and now. Pray that God would move in a special way over the services to come and that lives would be radically changed. Prayer can move mountains. Do not allow the size of a prayer meeting to dictate whether you should host them. Do your part by hosting a prayer meeting, and God will do his part in providing a blessing.

3 STEPS TO REACH THE COMMUNITY

(Pause, Pray, Participate)

The church seems to be in a perpetual decline for many mainline denominations. While some leading indicators show that the church is changing, I don't buy into the notion that the church must decline. In fact, "with God all things are possible" (Matt 19:26). If your local church struggles to reach the community, let me encourage you to pause, pray, and participate where God is leading. By joining with the community, the church can reconnect with lost people and help the people inside the church to see and meet their needs through Christ-love. Do not allow the discouragement of lack of attendance or community engagement to keep your church trapped in a cycle of mental decline. Through forward dreaming, the church will be able to connect with the community, and Christ will be honored for it.

Pause from the Busyness of Ministry to See Where God's Ministry Is Needed

There is a tendency to start something, anything, to save the church. But duplicating other community services in the community defeats the purpose. Think about it this way: the church can be so busy being the church that the members get caught up in church business and not the church's spiritual business. Let me say it another way: programs have taken over productive opportunities to reach people outside the four walls of the church. The question the church should ask is, How are we living out the call to be a church in the redemption business? Pause and reflect on that question by asking how your local church serves others? How do you serve others? How many have been saved, sanctified, and sent out to serve the kingdom in the past year or even five years?

If not many, pause and pattern yourself after God by seeking his will over the people's will. The church is not alive to perpetuate inside thinking but an outward gospel that dreams to reach the community around them.

When the church community takes a moment to pause and reflect on where God is leading, the church can adapt to the needs of the community and mobilize themselves to embody Christ. It's not just the responsibility of the pastor or church leaders; each and every one has a role to play in fulfilling God's mission. Church members must challenge each other to see Christ in the hard and out-of-the-way places in the community and go there to be a blessing to the community.

Pray for Opportunities to Serve People, Places, and for Future Partnerships

Prayer must become the central part of whatever the local church does. Two or three minutes of prayer time on a Sunday will not engage the church to obey its calling to reach the lost. Specific times of prayer (forty or twenty-one days of prayer and fasting, weekly prayer meetings, or even once-a-month prayer days) are better than doing nothing. By engaging God in prayer, the people will build a solid spiritual foundation that will undergird them through times of trouble and strengthen their faith. Prayer is not one and done, but a continual intentional focus that centers a person not on the worldly needs around them but the needs of God. Through reliance on God through prayer and scriptural reading, the church and its leaders will see where God calls them to serve.

Prayer will help position the church for the future. For struggling churches, prayer time is an afterthought to their dilemma. Instead of seeing prayer as a last resort, the church needs to move prayer to be the first resort of everything they do. Prayer can be the catalyst to renewal and can reawaken the outlook to reach the community. Find time to pray. As a church, dedicate specific times to pray throughout the church year. As a pastor or church leader, lead by example and seek God daily or hourly, spending time on dedicated prayer for the spiritual renewal of self and the local church. If the church is going to connect with the community, then it must be prayed up and ready to go through the spiritual warfare battles that will come with engaging the playground of the world with the gospel.

Participate Where God Leads the Local Church to Reach the Neighborhood Around the Church

While the church has been pushed to its brink in a post-Christian world, there is still hope where many seem hopeless. In each community, there are pockets of Jesus to be seen if the church is willing to embrace a community-centric model of serving. The model is built around people and existing programs where the church can come up alongside and serve. Think about it this way: Is there a school that needs reading buddies, a senior center that needs volunteers, or a clothing closet that needs donations? What may seem like small steps are giant steps in establishing a new service paradigm between the church and the community. God can use the church to connect in quintessential ways if it remains open for service opportunities. One of many ways to help the church connect with the community is by thinking and then participating where God is already in the community.

Here is an idea: put a map on a bulletin board and put a red pushpin in to show where the church is located within the map. Draw a one-mile circle around the church. That is the church's area of intentional focus. Find schools and nonprofit organizations within this intention zone, and mark them with yellow pushpins. Begin to strategize, through conversations with these potential partners, on how the church can help. When the church finds a willing partner, turn their pushpin from yellow to green. Then go and serve. The idea is not to spread the church too thin but to have it think through potential partnerships, find ways to embrace them, and serve with Christ-love and effectiveness.

As we shifted from stagnancy to renewal, the church board and I looked for early and easy wins everyone could cheer about.

Using Prayer to Focus the Church

These practical community connections would help us reinvest in the community through prayer and outreach, connecting us from the pew back into the streets with our neighbors.

Initiative 2025 is not just a win we needed but a beacon of hope. It's a journey that we're all part of, with three phases or areas that each of us could contribute to reach our community and demonstrate what's possible. In a season of decline, it's easy to forget that *trying* is trusting God with the church's future. So, try something! Anything that honors God and helps reignite the vision to reach the community for Jesus. Your role is crucial, and your efforts are what make this initiative a success. Whatever is possible is possible with God.

Here are the three things we tried early on:

1. Community Center—Open gym nights, expanded sports programs, Get Active Campaign (wellness focus for seniors).

2. PAC—Plant a parent-affiliated church at a nursing home area called a care campus.

3. Hero Days—Quarterly events to bless police, fire, EMS, city workers, and teachers.

So in early fall, just three months into our revitalization effort, we launched points two and three. Each was designed to reach different people and encourage congregation members to volunteer. We encouraged diversity in these efforts, ensuring that everyone could find a way to contribute. And the results were inspiring. Our local PAC started reaching eight to ten senior saints who could not attend church elsewhere. We saw firefighters and school personnel get blessed through prayer, encouragement, and monthly donut deliveries from church members. These may seem like small steps, but they were significant for our church, showing that everyone's involvement, no matter how small, is crucial for our renewal.

We celebrated these early wins repeatedly in our weekly bulletin, social media, and pulpit. Why? When a church declines, a defeatist attitude takes hold, and hope in doing something again sparks a renewal that can carry the congregation forward until new life springs up in the form of a new family, widower, or guest on a Sunday morning. Within that first year, Initiative 2025 brought hope and a new level of excitement to those who volunteered. While these are not all the steps to reach the community, it is a starting point as you embrace a new view to see the community and church connected.

WORSHIP THROUGH A TRANSITION SEASON

When change happens, members can either fight it or lean toward the challenges that have come forward. Leaning into the problem is a determination to find a solution to a problem that needs to be fixed in a way that honors the past but is forward-looking. The goal is to find a way forward and seek a pattern of evaluating the situation, reviewing what works and does not, and then addressing the issue so that it's a win for many.

Worship What Has Transpired

Maybe you have found yourself pausing and reflecting on the season that you are currently in or that just ended. Think back to the good things God brought about within the relationships that you are leaving. See the positive, even sometimes through the negative emotions. Capture in the light of day the brightness of your ministry experience on the people and community you have been a part of. In this place you are leaving, you can see God in the faces and people he brought to the church. You've laughed and cried, but through it all you were faithful. Faithful to the call. Devoted to the people. Loyal to serving where God had planted you. Celebrate what God has done through your ministry. As people left during the process of revitalization, some said very hurtful words about my preaching and leadership style. I chose to use their words as fuel to keep going forward. Maybe you felt that pain I just shared in your own ministry. Know this truth: you have sowed well into the local church and deserve to worship what God did or is doing through revitalization. Celebrate the saved and the lost ones who came home, baptisms, baby dedications, and new members or even the kind word spoken. In my desk, I keep a series of handwritten notes and cards that people have given me during the transition time. On hard days, I would review them to remind myself that God had called me to this place. Even if some wanted me to leave. Celebrate the places where God used you to help the church transition from the past to the present with an eye toward the future.

Worship what has transpired. The time you have devoted yourself to is not lost on those who have seen your love for others and your heart for Jesus. What has occurred during your service (current or former) has not been lost on those you impacted with the gospel. They have heard the gospel message. They have seen the words mirrored through your actions, and they will carry forth your example into the future with them.

Worship God in the Season You Find Yourself In

When change comes to the pastoral front door in the form of negative words from a member, it fills the pastor with such emotion it's almost hard to breathe. Through various emotions, the pastor has to say goodbye to what was, for what is to come. Like a herder with his sheep, you have felt the bite of the one you were called to guide and protect.

> Just 16% of Americans say religion is the most important thing in their life, according to a new report released this week by the Public Religion Research Institute. A 2020 survey found that the average congregation size across Christian denominations is less than half what it was in 2000—down to 65 from 137. It also found that on average, a third of churchgoers are 65 or older, twice that age group's representation in the general population. These numbers held true for Protestants, Evangelicals, and Catholics alike. Only congregations of other faith

traditions—including Islam, Baha'i and Judaism—are seeing increases, the survey said.[1]

You have lost sleep praying and worrying about conversations spoken, words exchanged, or the lack thereof. You have fought the fight and come out the other side wiser for it. Serving God is more than just preaching on Sunday mornings. It is visiting the sick, addressing sin, preaching the gospel, and staying faithful to your life's calling.

In this hour of uncertainty beyond the move of where you find ministry, worship God for helping you overcome the obstacles that you have been through or are in the midst of. Celebrate how you have grown as a pastor and, more importantly, as a faithful follower of Christ. Spend some time reflecting not on the battles themselves but on the victories that came through sincere prayer, encouragement from the saints, and love from your spouse. See the hand of God as he guided you through this season. With that openness to obeying God, you have stayed faithful and now move forward into uncharted territory, stronger because of your devotion.

---

1. Neuman, "Faithful."

Chapter 4

Do the Work Today for Success Tomorrow

As a pastor, leader, or active church member, you want to see your local church filled with smiling, happy faces of all generations. However, the reality for many small to mid-size churches is that they struggle to get their regular attendees, much less new guests, to attend more than twice a month on average. All one must do is go to any major internet marketing site, and you can find countless books, articles, and podcasts produced on turning around the local church. Each of the writers, me included, writes from a perspective of what has happened or is happening within their local context, and the work must be seen as not a silver bullet approach but a long-term view of how, through microsteps, the church can begin to turn around.

I wish each church would receive one silver bullet that would instantly transform the church without anyone leaving or getting mad. That is not the case. Before I arrived at the church to become the pastor, I delved into the data of the past and present of the church. Our denomination collects data yearly in many areas, including worship attendance, finances, baptisms, conversions, etc., and the data I reviewed revealed the plight of the church God had called me to. What had to be figured out early, and then often over time, was what success looked like for a dying church. Was it just staying alive to fight another day? Was it the number of people in the seats on average each Sunday? Or how many touchpoints church members made with the community over the past month? Was it the biblical mandate focused on conversions and baptismal rates year over year? Whatever definition of success we might have had, it was going to take work.

I have always said that people may mislead you, but the numbers never lie. What the numbers said about the church was that the church was in trouble. With a decline of 60.04 percent in worship attendance in the last decade on top of thirteen straight years of financial decline, a turnaround would take time. The reality was that many ignored these numbers, made excuses, or did not comprehend how much trouble the church was in. Change was not happening for change's sake but to save the church. The church the members loved was sick, but they would not acknowledge they (the church) were sick. So where was the hope? Hope came in the form of the leadership team, a group of dedicated individuals who were integral to the church's future. The support your leadership team provides in the face of negative voices from others is essential in the face of those who have withheld tithes, or who left the church over the changes.

As a leader in the local church, you should understand that doing the work today is for success tomorrow. The seeds you plant in a person's life will bear fruit in God's timing. When you focus on long-term solutions rather than short-term fluctuations and capture the imagination of what could be, God's success will come. Let me caution you on the definition of success; when I write about success, it's not about numbers or business metrics but about lives impacted and changed through the word of God.

Focus on Long-Term Solutions

When you find yourself in a struggling church, it's natural to feel the urge to make quick changes, point fingers, and avoid personal responsibility. However, instead of casting blame, let's focus on

Do the Work Today for Success Tomorrow

what we can control, with God's power working through us. It may seem counterintuitive to think about long-term solutions when the church is facing spiritual, membership, and financial challenges. But it's in these moments, when we come together and unite our efforts, that God can truly begin to help the church rebound.

Imagine you're a church with no children attending. It might seem futile to invest in a children's program, decorate a room, put on a fresh coat of paint, replace the carpet, purchase supplies, and secure a teacher. But with a long-term focus, you're not just preparing for the future, you're setting the stage for God to show up and bless the church as the people pray. Many churches and their leaders forget that God wants us to partner with him, serving our part in the grander service to the church and community. A real-world example of not doing anything, or waiting until it's too late, is what happened with the Kansas university system, which has spent nearly seventeen million dollars to knock down buildings to save eighty million dollars in deferred maintenance repairs. "We can't spend all our increased funding just for building maintenance," Wint Winter, a member of the Board of Regents, shared. "We have an obligation to identify all the unmet spending needs in the universities."[1] The article goes on to report from the Kansas Board of Regents Facilities Director Chad Bristow that "when you have a lot of deferred maintenance, you have a lot of surprises. It wouldn't be prudent to not have some money set aside for emergency issues."[2] The church can ill afford waiting on people and funding before they develop a God-given plan to turn around the church. So instead of waiting on people, why not partner with God through prayer, direction, and obedience to the call he has placed on the local church? Do not be a church that waits for blessings but one that actively seeks to bless our communities in obedience to God's calling daily.

Let me give you five key suggestions for long-term planning that have helped my church:

1. Carpenter, "Kansas Universities."
2. Carpenter, "Kansas Universities."

1. **Pray and Ask:** Seek God's face through corporate prayers of forgiveness, wisdom, and discernment about the church's current and future plans.

2. **Go and Find:** Find areas where God draws the church into the community or community groups who want to partner with the church through the use of space agreements on the church campus.

3. **Obey and Do:** Follow God's will by designing programs and partnerships that challenge the people to leave the pew and serve others.

4. **Be and Act:** The world is challenging followers to serve in darkness. Be light in the dark and shine the goodness (God) into the community.

5. **Bless and Maintain:** Serve with an eye toward a long-term commitment to adapt and change while keeping Christ at the center of service in and out of the church. Everything the church does is to see lives changed.

These keys are ideals to strive towards. They should be used as a benchmark to establish new work by seeking innovative ways to leverage church resources, like empty spaces, and adapt them for community use. Think about serving as Christ by working with partners or people who may not share the church's values. It's a tall order, but it's one that God has challenged the church to fulfill.

Capture the Imagination of What Is to Come

When I serve alongside churches and leaders navigating a challenging season, I am reminded of the crucial role the local leader plays. As we walk the space in person or through Zoom, I begin to listen to the echoes of the past, understanding that God is preparing a new thing to emerge if the local church will trust him. The notion that everything must remain unchanged is diminished when the pastor and lay leaders entrust the future of the church to God and begin to envision what it could become. As a leader

Do the Work Today for Success Tomorrow

guiding the church out of decline, you must skillfully balance the present with future needs. Let me provide you with three strategies to ignite the imagination of what lies ahead.

1. **Develop a Strategic Plan:** Envisioning the future of the church is not enough. You need to develop a strategic plan to turn that vision into reality. Think about where you want the church to be in six months, one year, three years, and five years from now. Then, develop a step-by-step plan to do the "big" and "small" things to get there. This will take visionary leadership and tenacity not to give up when things get complicated.

2. **Keep Your Focus on God's Vision for the Local Church:** Let his vision guide and inspire you to move the church forward. Share what God has shown you during your prayer time with others through sermons, personal conversations, and teachings so that they too catch the vision.

3. **You are Not a Lone Ranger Christian:** It will take a team to overcome the obstacles that the church faces today. Remember, as a leader, you are not alone in this journey. You have a team of dedicated prayer warriors who are ready to support you, endorse your efforts, speak positively in public, and encourage you personally. But you have to ask for support and help. The support of these pew leaders is crucial in honoring the call and keeping the focus on Jesus and others while supporting the efforts.

These steps will not only help achieve the new focus but also provide the motivation to keep pressing forward during the process of renewal. God has an amazing plan for your church and ministry. So ask yourself, will I do the work today for success tomorrow, or wait on someone else to obey God's call?

REASONS TO BECOME A CHURCH REVITALIZER

Throughout the latter half of the last decade, a spiritual wind has refocused pastoral leadership to reevaluate the established church.

Once, pastors would not want to take a church that was struggling or in most cases, dying. Today, there is a new breed of ministers who are taking up the challenge to help revitalize the local church. I believe God is thankful for those ministers called into the arena of church revitalization. The work that is done is done to the glory of God as he helps reshape the local church into a vibrant church that reaches its neighbors with the gospel.

Are you called? Are you questioning the call on your ministry from the pulpit to the pew or vice versa? You are not alone. Let me help you think through this process through a series of thoughts.

Established Churches Need Vision, Leadership, and Clear Direction

Study after study has shown that most evangelical churches in North America are in some state of decline. With decreasing membership, aging buildings, deferred maintenance, and lack of community engagement, the church has seen its numbers reduce. St. John's United Church of Christ in Columbus, Ohio, faced the conflict with determination to do something. "We were left with the stark choice: choose to 'die happy' and run out of remaining cash in our budget until we ultimately closed the doors, or sell to the highest bidder and design a new future for our congregation less dependent on our church building."[3] The idea of dying and not fighting was not what they were going to do. It takes a tenacious leader to stand up to the doom and gloom and choose to fight for God's plan. The demoralized people need a strong leader who has passion to save the church, the lost, and to revive its members.

While some outlier churches have seen an increase in attendance and community engagement, most are facing a crisis moment to either reengage or close the local church. The concept of a church hiring a younger pastor as the silver bullet is misguided but sought often by churches who are in decline. The sad truth is that there are not enough younger pastors in the pipeline to fill all the

---

3. Bauman, "Beyond the Legacy."

pulpits opening in the next ten years as Baby Boomers continue to retire and the early wave of Generation X begins to leave the pulpits for retirement.

The established church needs visionary pastors who see what could be, not where the local church finds itself today in a state of decline. The revitalizer's role is to help the church capture where it finds itself today and lead it into a new future defined not by programs but by the needs of people in the shadow of the steeple. The revitalizer will help the church reengage the community, embrace community needs, and overlay those needs in a spiritual context that embraces where the church finds the marketplace. This role is exciting yet challenging and will need a person with a clear vision and discernable leadership qualities that will help, not force, an established church to become a church back on a mission with God.

Established Churches Need a Fresh Perceptive to Reach the Community Around Them

As you drive throughout your community, begin to see the picture of who the community is and where it needs to go. By evaluating the needs seen around you, you can better understand the community culture and the complex nature of returning to the church and to the streets to meet its neighbors. For many in the established church, everything around them has changed except the church. Thus, any change brought to the church is met with pushback from those members holding on to the last vestige of the past. A church revitalizer enters the church community, understanding that they are called not to deconstruct the local church but to reconstruct the hopes and dreams of those members still sitting in the pew. Through observation, conversations, and relationships, the revitalizer guides the church into a new season in the church's life by listening to members' fears and faith. Leaning into these stories, of where God was and is at work, can help them recapture the God dreams they have for the local church.

Through a fresh outlook ladened with positive antidotes and encouraging celebrations highlighting small and large wins, the revitalizer can provide new opportunities for the church and community to connect. These connection times are about drawing in new members rather than drawing out current members to serve in the community. Only after the revitalizer has laid the foundation can the church build community relationships. Take your time with this step, as this step lays the groundwork for future blessings.

Established Churches Have Incredible Legacies That Need Redeeming for This Generation

When a revitalizer comes to a church for the first time, they must realize that God has worked inside the church for decades. They know that changing something out of hand might be so destructive that it terminates their ministry before it really begins. Instead, they become the church's leading historian, understanding the past to reengage the past with the present. The history of a local church is not to be buried but honored. Why do you think there are all the nameplates and plaques around a church? It is about celebrating the heroes of the church who strived to serve God and the local church faithfully. Honoring the past and the people connected to it should be done in a way that captures the moment the church is living in. Develop a legacy room or living museum in your lobby where you can share the past, through pictures, awards, and stories, by connecting it to God's new future for the local church.

WHAT TYPE OF LEADER ARE YOU

Leading a church is challenging, but with the advent of social media and cell phones, leadership traits that could have been hidden for years are exposed to a larger crowd today. Today, members and the community closely watch pastoral leadership under a microscope. The pastor's leadership style can create a nurturing place to grow in faith or a toxic environment that fosters unhealthy relationships. The ability to more closely align with the leadership traits of Jesus makes a pastor more effective in reaching others. If you are not a pastor but a layperson in the church, these same traits are seen in members, so review them and decide how you will react to others.

Ivory Tower Leader

We have all been there, where we received directions from a leader and quickly realized they had needed more information before making that decision, and they would have responded differently if they'd had it. An ivory tower leader leads from the office desk and views things from a thirty thousand-foot level without asking for suggestions or listening to other people's thoughts. This type of leadership might be the most dangerous leadership style in the church because it relies on one person's judgment to make all the decisions, which might not have all the information. After all, they do not ask others for their opinion. Sadly, this leadership style has been seen countless times over the decades due to large church scandals. Each time, the pastoral leader needed an inner circle of subordinates who could have spoken truth into this leader's life.

Whiteboard Leader

Churches desperately want a leader who helps them overcome their obstacles. A whiteboard leader is seen as a futuristic leader who sees the problem before the church, evaluates needs, reviews all dimensions of the past, present, and future needs, and begins to draw up ideas to solve the church's problems. The whiteboard leader might have so many ideas that some fall to the wayside because they lack focus on the main issue before the church. Having a strong supporting cast around this type of leader helps them focus on the task by narrowing the problems they are facing and being guided long-term by the original vision, but with a visionary team that can work backward to complete the task on the task dream wish list. Without a team, the leader will not trust or listen.

The leader will become disjointed in thinking and could miss the overall mark.

Consensus Leader

This type of leader wants to make everyone happy and is willing to lose their voice. In a world that is polarized in many ways, this leader tries to find the middle ground for every considerable agreement that needs to be made in the church. The consensus leader will slow down the process to ensure everyone feels heard, seen, and valued. Along the way, the leader will deal with strong personalities that try to dictate the conversation and will have to be willing to veer the decision-making back to the center to garner a larger vote share in the decision process. The downside of a consensus leader is that nothing gets done beyond hosting meetings and talking about projects almost to their death. When a church urgently finds itself in a significant decline, this type of leader could harm the process and sink the church by talking and not doing.

Compassionate Leader

Jesus led through the example of humble teaching, living, praying, and seeking out others who might not have felt a part of the leadership team. The compassionate leader leads by following the principles of Jesus, striving to obtain a higher calling in their ability as a leader by living like Jesus. This type of leader is seen by others as approachable, a good listener, and one who challenges the status quo by trying to include everyone in the process. The negative side of this type of leadership is that compassion sometimes overtakes the logistical needs that the church is facing, which may delay long-term decision-making for short-term compassion, thus having compassion rather than a passion to complete the project.

Community Leader

This type of leader sees the community not separate from the church but as a part of what the church is. Community leaders value the needs and voice of the neighbors around the church and strive to connect the two (neighborhood and church). This is seen through the community center model church that values people and interactions over Sunday liturgical teachings. The leader sees through Jesus' eyes the needs around the church and strives to reach them by using the church campus as an extension of Christ's hands and feet to reach the lost.

Each of these five leadership traits has positives and negatives as a stand-alone model. But when a leader uses portions of these to lead in the local church, the church is better for it. Spend some time reflecting on your current leadership model by writing down the pluses and minuses of where your leadership stands on paper, and see if tweaks could be made to make you a more effective leader. If you are a layperson reading this book and serve in the local church, these leadership styles are seen in the pew also. Let me encourage you to go back and strike the word "pastor" and insert your name, and see where you fall into this pattern of leadership as you reflect on what you have read.

OVERCOMING THE SMALL CHURCH MINDSET

How many are you running? It is a question that pastors love to ask each other. While the median church in North America is sixty-five people, pastors seem to forget what God can do through a small church.[4] As Sunday numbers increase, the likelihood of the local church getting noticed by outsiders or denominational officials does not tell the whole story of how God is using the church in North America to make a difference in lives of community members. *Increase does not equate to church health or spiritual growth.* Underline and highlight that sentence. Then go back and read it again while you allow the words to sink in.

4. Earls, "Small Churches."

Be honest with yourself, the local church is not built on megachurches but small, out-of-the-way churches whose pastors give it their all, by serving bi-vocationally. The local church is built around a small cluster of families per church who sacrifice all to keep the local church operating. In essence the small church is just a mindset and not a reality, as the "small church" is the average-sized church in North America and in the community you serve.

Small Does Not Mean Ineffective

In the corporate world, having a small ratio of attendees and limited growth year over year is ineffective leadership. However in the kingdom mindset, year-over-year relationship building is seen as deepening a discipleship culture that will strengthen the church's foundational footings, preparing it to nurture long-term relationships that will enhance the local church and positively impact the local community for decades. Any church can create a sensation, but churches that create a Christ-centered church create long-term disciple-makers, who in turn make disciples who impact the world.

Let me be honest: I envy the pastor or layperson who serves one church for their whole ministry (pulpit or pew) because they can do life with people. What an opportunity! They get to witness couples falling in love and getting married. They watch families grow from two to three in celebrating life through a birth. They have the privilege of remembering those who finish their race on earth and rejoice in heaven as they officiate over a funeral of a departed saint of the church. Serving in a small church is a life-impacting ministry, and only eternity will know the difference the ministry made. The effectiveness of ministry cannot be measured in people in the pews only, but in lives transformed by the touchpoints imparted on the community through personal relationship through the local church. God uses all sizes of churches to affect their community through the effectiveness of faithful followers, who believe in his word and live it out daily. Small churches are effective churches who are part of God's plan for the local community.

Small Does Not Mean Culturally Irrelevant

For many, the small church has been seen on the movie screen of Hollywood as a backward or backwoods ministry, when it truly is life-changing for those who walk through its doors. Where once size mattered with building size, auditorium seat count, and larger-than-life programs, in today's culture relationships matter.

With the world seemingly more interconnected through technology, it has become disconnected from personal and professional relationships that go beyond the surface. This vast ocean between connection and disconnection has left the culture yearning for togetherness. What an opportunity for the small church. The church allows the disconnected to find a link through small groups, meaningful relationships that develop through fellowship times, and a deeper connection beyond the superficial Sunday hellos. God has created the church to connect to the disconnected through a meaningful relationship with Christ through the small church, creating an opportunity to make the local church more culturally relevant to the needs of today. Instead of fretting about the small mindset inside the local church, embrace who God has created you to be and be more proactive in providing opportunities to go deeper with your church family.

Lean into the society that has cast people from the dinner table to hide behind the keyboard and screen. See the opportunity to interact with people one-on-one over a meal, coffee, or conversation about life. Feel free to develop small groups that connect to people's interests, such as a book club, sports outing, or young parents club. Let me say, whatever you do, focus on the relational aspect of connecting and living out Christlikeness daily through your interactions. Don't apologize for being a small church; focus on being a community for a lost neighbor.

Small Does Not Mean Less Than

The work you do serving in your local church is God-valued work that makes an eternal difference in the lives of those you impact. If you were to add up all the people you have impacted through your ministry, you would be humbled by the God count. But I bet, if you are like most pastors or laypeople, you get caught up on the count of how many come each Sunday instead of the lives impacted on the other six days of the week. It is humbling to realize that God did not call you to be a counter of sheep but to be a herder of sheep.

God has not forgotten your ministry or your local church. He sees the work you are sowing into the community. He considers the preparation time for each sermon and lesson taught on Wednesday night. He is not blind by your service but is not bound to build a large church for you to serve in. He has called you to live a faithful life that honors him, not an awarded one for church growth. It is humbling to realize that God uses you despite your desires. The value of your ministry cannot be found in the numbers placed on a tick sheet at the end of the service for you to review but in the lives who heard your message, not in words but in deeds. Through their daily walk, God uses small church pastors and lay leaders alike to impact the local church and community. A small pastorate does not mean less than. See it as more opportunities to share Jesus with the larger community outside the church's walls through daily interactions of the pastor and church members in the community.

If you serve in a small church, know this truth: you are not alone. Your work each week is effective, culturally relevant, and means more than you know to the people you interact with.

REDEEMING THE CHURCH FOR CHRIST

Traditionally, summer in the local church is a time to relax before ramping back up when fall returns. The prolific hymn writer Fanny J. Crosby wrote the lyrics to "Redeemed, How I Love to Proclaim It!" in 1882. The chorus of this well-known hymn says, "Redeemed by the blood of the lamb! Redeemed thro' His infinite mercy—His child, and forever, I am."[5] As you evaluate your local church, do not

---

5. Crosby, "Redeemed," stanza 1.

see the issues; see the one who can help redeem the problems and turn them into an altar of glory for God.

Summer is an excellent time for your church to redeem a room piled with items for a future classroom for children, but you do not have to wait for summer, or any season for that matter, to start. Reevaluate programs to see if they meet the current or future needs. Instead of fretting over change, see it as a way to redeem what God wants for your ministry and the local church. Do not allow "stuff" to get in the way of the future. That stuff once was *for* the future. A future program, class, or ministry. But today it's become a collection of "old" things that cannot be restored but could, if cleared out, prepare the space for a new future. There are three ways you can redeem the local church: by redeeming the vision, space, and community connection.

Redeem the Vision

When a church finds itself in a crisis, the glory days mentality takes hold. Typically, a tiny remnant of believers holds on in search of clear direction and guidance from a faithful pastor. They in turn take their spiritual eyes off the call God has placed on the church, and hopes in humanity. When was the last time your local church discussed the mission or vision statement? Many churches had not revised the words since before . . . You add in the date. I bet it's a long time. Spend some time refreshing the commitment to the call, and how the community of believers wants to connect with the community, by updating the statements to fit the new season in the church's life. If you do not know where you are going, how do you plan to help the church get there? That is why seeds of vision are built on what you do today rather than tomorrow.

Allow the vision to drive the process of revamping the church culture by shining a light on the mission of who the church is called to be. It's an incredible opportunity to speak of God's fresh vision for the church.

Redeem the Space

Traditionally, churches have large empty spaces that were filled with children and families but have now become closed-off areas or worse, storage rooms that are never cleaned out. The once-large footprint seen as a growth area has become an albatross around the necks of declining churches as deferred maintenance issues have piled up, which force already financially strapped churches to make tough choices. Instead of seeing these spaces as lost to the history of the past, reimagine the area as a computer room for adult education classes, incubators for future startup businesses that rent out space for offices, or even shared space with another church.

An example of seeing space with an eye toward a new vision is that we used to run a local market radio and television ministry in the 1980s and '90s. The church built rooms to record, edit, and host broadcasts as part of that vision. Since the church no longer uses that space for a studio, it has been used primarily as storage for various items. Instead of allowing the space to hold Christmas trees and other items, what if we used it for a podcast studio to be opened to the community to share their talents? Or even a production studio where streamers can share their video gaming skills. The idea is to find creative ways to connect the church and community as one.

Redeeming unused space is about reclaiming what was lost for what could be with God's help. No program, order of service, or room should be off limits to evaluation by those who want to see the church redeemed for God's glory. Challenge yourself to find one program or space and dream about what it could be and who you hope to reach. The challenge is not in redeeming the area but in reclaiming the glory of God for what he wants to happen in the future.

Do the Work Today for Success Tomorrow

Redeem the Community

Change is constant in the world in which the church ministers. As the community has changed, the leadership should ask, Has the church adapted to the culture or contextualized the experiences it finds itself in? The church is not called to live in the world but to find ways to infiltrate the community with the gospel of Jesus Christ. As the church leadership evaluates the current and future needs of the church, begin to see where God is currently working and lead your people there. There is no need to recreate programs God already uses within the community. However, are there areas where the community could use the church's help, passion, and leadership? If yes, that is where the church goes into action. What an opportunity to redeem the faltering community around the church by the church setting its sights on reinvesting in community relationship building, compassionate ministries, and intergenerational relationships within the neighborhood. Many cities need religious leaders to use their connections to help lift the community, through investments in reading programs, park cleanups, and volunteering at the senior center.

Nearly three decades later, the homeless ministry, dubbed His Mission, was ebbing and flowing from year to year but did not change much. The community and neighborhood around the church had changed. The church had changed, but the His Mission ministry did not. The mission and vision of His Mission, to feed the needs of homeless men and women spiritually and physically, marched on with little oversight from the church board. What was birthed out of the plight of homelessness for a church member transformed into a ministry that has impacted thousands. Looking at the ministry from the outside, I saw it excelling at the mission (feeding others spiritually and physically). It was natural to see the evolution of this ministry into something more significant in the future. If all ministry partners would catch the future-forward vision, this ministry and others could impact more people with the gospel. A little background to the story was that prior to coming to this assignment, I spent four years as a bi-vocational pastor, serving as the executive director of a soup kitchen in another state that fed over twenty-three thousand meals on average each year along with giving away over three thousand food boxes to individuals in need. I saw instantly that I could help this ministry, and the church would be able to help more people. The ministry had used the gym for decades to feed and host services, but we had an opportunity to use two former duplexes, which at one time housed a Spanish congregation, as the new site of this combined ministry. With more space, they would have a real opportunity to lean into food insecurity, a major issue in our city.

Can I say that for those attempting revitalization in a church, it is hard to change a ministry or even adapt one that has thirty years of history. To determine where the church would be headed in the future, it was necessary to achieve the broader goal of focusing on compassion, community, and Christian education as outreach points. Within seven months of my arrival, the church board married the two ministries with similar paths (His Mission and Naz Thrift Store) under a new compassionate ministry center approved by our denomination. For ten years, the church operated a thrift store with an independent board that was separate from the church. Most of the thrift store board were non-church members, most of them former members. To close one chapter and open another, the thrift store board had to be dissolved, and the church board, acting as the new corporation board, took the lead—more on that story in the closing chapters. But for now, bringing these two ministry programs under one umbrella was a goal through a compassion ministry center. It seemed easy, but nothing in revitalization is ever easy.

The struggle over independence and who directed the vision of the new compassionate ministry center was a spiritual battle more than a disagreement in direction. Spiritually, there were people, who had left the church, who were stirring the pot through damaging false accusations. Some current members held tightly to their golden idols in trying to keep the ministries unchanged. These words seem harsh, but believe me, it was a painful chapter in the church's life and my ministry. I was personally maligned, lied about, accused of things I never did, and left hung out to dry by members who smiled in my face and spoke evil behind my back. Thankfully, most members and the church board constantly backed the vision, stuck it out when it got rough, and pushed back against the falsehoods. They understood as I did: this was spiritual warfare because the church was going to take more territory in the future for the kingdom. Understand that you cannot take it personally when things are said against you or the vision God has given the church. You must keep your head down, keep prayed up, and trust that in the process God will guide you through the distractions and into the promise of future growth.

Chapter 5

A Five-Year Cycle to Church Revitalization

DR. NINA GUNTER, GENERAL superintendent emeritus in the Church of the Nazarene, said, "The church is not in crisis. It remains in Christ."[1] The story of the legacy church is one of large buildings, multiple programs, and staff. The legacy church was a hub for Christian life from schools, childcare centers, and sports leagues to hosting major concerts. Over time, with the cultural shift, the Christian church believed that if they built it, the people would come. With time, that spiritual gamble did not pay off. Today, many former grand church properties sit half empty, deferred maintenance has taken most of the operating budget, and the population of churchgoers is aging faster than the rate of new, younger converts. Regardless of the denomination, the story of the legacy church is the same: fighting to stay alive.

The period of inaction has long passed. The local church was challenged to fight for its spiritual life. If the church was to rebound from decline, it would take the leadership and members getting back to the fundamentals of Christianity, which is to serve others. Share the gospel, and spend time investing in others and the community. As a pastor who is leading a legacy church back

---

1. Church of the Nazarene, "GA2013."

A Five-Year Cycle to Church Revitalization

from the brink of death, I write from experience, not academic conjecture. I have found that through a cycle of revitalization, the church is slowly rebounding from the onset of sudden death back to life. Suppose your local church is like more than 75 percent of churches, regardless of denomination, averaging less than sixty-five people each Sunday.[2] In that case, the cycle to revitalization focus might help your church refocus on the mission that God has called your local church to. If you want a tool to revitalize your church, this cycle will help you get there.

Year One: Stabilization

As you approach the first year of reviving the church, the focus should not be on winning new guests but on slowing the decline of existing members by loving the people you have, not dreaming of the people you wish you had. The first year of any revitalization effort is one of the most challenging because you have to help the church shift its focus from an inward posture to preparing for future guests, while still holding on to the members you currently have. Your actions in year one will hinder or help the process as you move forward. Do not skip this step or think you can breeze through. If you fail to build a strong foundation in year one, it will all come crashing down around you before you end the revitalization cycle.

As you begin to invest in loving the people you have, you must start to evaluate where the church finds itself. The evaluation period is about connecting the vision of the church with the infrastructure of the church. For instance, does your parking lot look more like a sandlot than a parking area? Or are the carpets in the children's room so stained that it makes it look like an impressionist painting? Begin to see the church with guests' eyes, or ask someone who does not go to the church to review the church. Do not dismiss this view of the church; write down the needs and concerns and envision a new way forward. By reviewing the church's

---

2. Earls, "Small Churches."

infrastructure, you can develop a plan of action to repair, replace, and renew what could harm the future growth prospects of the church. Keep the focus on something other than cost: future guests who will visit.

Year Two: Strategize

As you embrace the realities the church has found itself in, do not hesitate to strategize how best to move forward. Year two is about building the structure to strengthen the church as you rebound from years of neglect and decline. This stage is about moving the church from an inward posture to an outward ministry-minded focus that enables the church to see past the current realities well into the future. As the church begins to dream again, leaders will start to see the current needs and things that will have to be addressed in the future to reach the community like never before. A word of caution: people might wonder why more people are not attending during this stage. Leaders must be open to explaining that with years, sometimes decades, of decline, people will not come back overnight or because of one event. It will take prayer, consistent community-mindedness, and dedicated focus on keeping the vision in front of the members. In this stage, there will be pushback from some who try to hold on to how things have always been. As a leader, you are called to help navigate these shifting times by focusing on the long-term health and well-being of the church.

As you focus more on outside the church, the leaders will have to evaluate the church budget, staffing needs, and programmatic offerings inside the church. During this challenging step, tough conversations are had through the evaluation of data-driven decision-making. Reviewing the future-forward budget (sometimes called zero-based budgeting), reviewing all staffing positions for current and future needs, and focusing on programs that fit the new vision to reach the community, the church leadership begins to see where God is taking the church. By reviewing programs, people, and positions inside the church, hard choices will have to be made. In this stage, this proverbial stop-kicking the spiritual can down the road will take place as the leaders begin to address the real needs the church is facing. Year two is a hard but foundational year that will either propel the church forward or leave it behind.

Year Three: Strategic

Leaders will spend more time preparing the church for future guests than receiving guests in the first two years of the revitalization effort. In year three, the work begins to pay off as the church seeks to assist partners in the community through service opportunities with nonprofits. Developing partners outside the church's walls allows the church to turn members' faith into action as they move to bless the community. The role of the leadership during this stage is to identify partnerships that could benefit both parties. As the church moved through the strategizing phase, they would have identified areas of the church campus that were underutilized: what space could be used by an outside agency, or other opportunities to use redirected budgeted resources to leverage toward beneficially connecting each side. The redirection cannot be done haphazardly but through open meetings where all stakeholders within the church can dream with the leadership about where they would like to see the church go. In these "dream sessions," the church begins to see the opportunity to bless the community creatively. The old mantra of "build it and they will come" will be turned on its head with "go" and "serve." The church's role will move from serving self to serving others.

As the church develops a strategic plan for reaching the community, it must review its current programs. Many legacy churches offered programmatic cafeteria-style selection, but with limited people and resources, those programs must be cut back to fit current needs. After the review, the enhancement of the leftover programs should be forward-looking and bent towards reaching new people with the gospel of Christ. If the church is going to rebound, it must reinvest in reaching new people and provide programs that sustain its spiritual development and interest.

Year Four: Sustain

Year four marks a year of rest and renewal. For the last three years, the church has been moving fast to turn around the slump of decline. Believe me, the church will want to slow down and sustain what they have accomplished. In this stage, the leadership begins to evaluate all areas (programs, positions, people, partnerships, and infrastructure) and adapt for mission creep. Mission creep is when the church leadership gets comfortable with where they are, and some will want to pull the church back to where it had moved forward from because everyone is tired of change. Do not fall into a comfortable mindset that could erase what the church has already accomplished. The goal in this stage is consistent progress toward reaching the community by doing the current things with excellence, with no significant projects or initiatives. Maintain what has been done in the previous years and dream for what could be in the future.

By sustaining the progress the church has accomplished in previous years, it has laid a new foundation to embrace the new season in ministry it finds itself in. This is an exciting time because progress can be seen and new opportunities await if the church is willing to embrace what is to come by preparing to do its part today. Through prayer, vision recasting, and a willingness to see the needs of gospel opportunities in the neighborhood, the church chooses to bless the community, not expecting anything in return.

Year Five: Success

As the revitalization cycle comes to completion, keep yourself from thinking the process is over. The cycle is just beginning again. It is time to start to dream again for the next five-year cycle. Restarting allows new ideas to percolate and partnerships to be developed to enhance what has already been developed in the last five-year process. By using the previous experiences and the data connected to the change accomplished in the last five years, the church begins to derive new future outcomes. Planning and progress will strengthen what is currently a part of the church and see the opportunities that the church has not yet fulfilled.

In year five, the church celebrates the success of the changes that have come about. The community of believers has changed, and new converts have been won through gospel-centered partnerships that have shown that the church cares for its neighbors. The church is willing to adapt to the culture around it while holding to the foundational teachings of Christ. A Christ-centered church has been resurrected where once a dying one lay dormant, waiting for closure. The ability of the church's leadership to celebrate the past, review the present, and dream towards the future creates an opportunity for God to bless the church. In return, the church blesses the community for decades to come, and it becomes a win-win for the church and community.

LEADING THE KAIZEN WAY

I first heard the word *kaizen* in my first year of high school, but it originated much earlier in the 1940s, post-WWII Japan, as manufacturers looked to restart and improve on what was lost during the war. The word kaizen, loosely translated into English to mean "change for the better" or, by its more formal understanding, "continuous improvement," has been used in the business and academic arenas for decades. However, it is a word that best describes many churches embarking on church revitalization, developing more robust discipleship programs, and winning new people to Jesus. Whatever the need, the Kaizen philosophy could help redeem what seems broken or hopeless in many ways.

In a church world looking for a quick fix to declining measurements, the local church leadership can utilize the Kaizen method to identify, analyze, create, evaluate, and celebrate the church's systems (programs, position, and partnerships) for continuous improvement. At the same time, you can use the Kaizen philosophy to help rebound and redefine how the local church will minister in the future.

Step 1: Identify the Problem for Improvement

There are seasons in the church's life when you want to throw your hands up as a leader and ask, What am I doing wrong? I know for me, I have felt it even amid my present turnaround. By identifying the problem for improvement, you are naming the issue publicly so that others can begin to develop a solution that leads the church forward. Leading the local church can be lonely, and it should not be. The idea of continuous improvement is built around everyone having a voice to help improve (programs, positions, or partnerships). It empowers everyone, from the pastor to the pew, to help in turning around the local church through a positive vision and voice. This idea is a significant shift for many, as many church members see it as the pastor's job to rebuild the children's program, visit the senior saints in the hospital, win new converts, etc.

As you begin the Kaizen process, identify one main issue that the team wants to address. Once that is agreed upon, begin to see the positives and negatives of the current program, position, or partnership by deciding where the church wants to improve. Think about it this way: Is it eliminating a program, providing more resources to an area, fixing up a new space, etc.? As the team identifies the problem, they can begin to dream of the future.

Step 2: Analyze the Current Situation for Quality

The problem has been publicly named; now what? The team moves to seek improvement by analyzing the current issue, and looking for hidden gems that might have been overlooked in the downturn or are worth saving as part of the new plan, through a creative idea lab. The idea lab is where you put chart paper up on a board or wall and throw out ideas, regardless of how large or small the group is. The focus should be on diverse stakeholders such as staff, church board, influential leaders, and lay members. You can either do these as individual groups or all at once, mixing the group. The idea is that it enables others to see, review, and speak about proposed ideas in an informal setting. With any small or large group idea, identify ways to make it feel safe, where everyone's opinions and thoughts matter. Make sure the idea lab reviews data for key takeaways, is willing to experiment, and debates with the understanding that ideas matter more than who is right and wrong in this flushing-out stage.

The team should take their time exploring the next steps in the idea lab, where everyone can share their thoughts and then narrow them down, zeroing in on the next steps. Rushing into the situation without truly analyzing all facets of the issue will cause more heartache. So slow down, do the work, and seek the gems amid the muck. This step focuses on developing quality, not quantity. Ask yourself, What resources does the team need to improve or fix the problem? What does that look like regarding the budget or the people who might be a part of the turnaround? Identifying quality is a complex but necessary step. Do not skip over this, thinking your team is more innovative than the church down the street. The foundational work done in this step will help the church revamp and improve for a new generation of believers.

Step 3: Create Opportunities or Systems Through New Solutions

The team is now ready to develop a step-by-step action plan to renew the struggling area. From identifying to dreaming is an exciting part of the renewal process. The team gets to move the turnaround plan from the idea lab (behind-the-scenes conversations) into a safe incubator (front-facing), which can be tweaked over time as the church adjusts to the new reality. Setting a time frame for the new program, partnership, or redesigned position to be reviewed will help keep the team focused on the original premise, which was continuous improvement.

Allow the creativity and safety of the idea lab to tinker with a program, position, or partnership to help make it better for the future, not just now. Dreaming and then adapting those dreams to fit the current realities and resources will help keep a forward-leaning posture for the church. By creating healthy wins, the team will create forward momentum to show that change is better when done together.

Step 4: Evaluate the Effectiveness of the Improvement

There is a tendency to rest once the heavy lifting has been accomplished. To continually improve, the church must constantly refocus on quality. Change takes a lot out of a leader, but change was not the focus, Kaizen was, which is continuous improvement. The improvement cycle continues not when the plan is born but when tweaked repeatedly to make it the best action plan possible for the church. Begin within the first month of implementation to evaluate the effectiveness of the improvement. Be bold about questioning what is working and what is not working. It is easier to adapt a new program to a new reality than an old one with an old reality mindset.

If the team notices that something is not working, stop it, change it, or keep evaluating it for a period of time. Do not allow the team to be lulled into a false sense of complacency. Keep pressing, asking questions, reviewing, adapting, and then relaunch if you have to, but in all ways keep improving the product.

Step 5: Celebrate the Improvement but Continue to Review

Celebrate the win. I love celebrating, not with candles, streamers, and horns but by sharing what God has done in the church's life. Four months into the turnaround, on behalf of the leadership team, I formally announced Believe Again, our campaign of revitalization for the church. We promised updated information on what had already occurred every few weeks and months and encouraged people to save their original booklet announcing the campaign as a score card on progress. Using the weekly bulletin, social media, creative booklets with phases and checklists, along with sermons to highlight what had occurred created a buzz throughout the

A Five-Year Cycle to Church Revitalization

campus. These seemingly insignificant announcements reinforced the "good" things happening, even if a small group were troubled by the change. Remember, movement begets momentum, and I was trying to encourage folks before the discouragement reached them in the form of a busybody unhappy with the change or loss of their power base in the church. Celebrate that church members came together to acknowledge a problem, reviewed the situation honestly, designed new systems, tinkered with the plan, and birthed it through practical learning and sharing. The idea behind Kaizen was to never stop improving, and with this five-step plan, the local church can continue to achieve new heights over time. While this may have been a business and academic model, the Kaizen model fits into the local church if the leadership team is willing to share power, trust the people, and work the process, never settling for comfort.

Comfort is the enemy of the church, and Kaizen opposes it. The Kaizen cycle constantly looks forward to seeing how the program, position, or partnership could be improved even more over time. If your church is stagnant or struggling to reach the community, using the Kaizen model could help restructure it to live out the mission of winning others to Christ. The cycle of revitalization and Kaizen create a one-two punch that will help carry the church to victory.

FORWARD MOMENTUM THROUGH MICROSTEPS

In a struggling church that has faced years of decline in attendance, lack of children, and deferred maintenance issues, the leadership tends to look for a person, program, or partnership that can reverse the decline in an instant. The Hail Mary hire or programmatic change is a desperate attempt to reverse decline. Maybe I was the Hail Mary hire. Or maybe the church board was looking for a radical change from the past. Either way, programmatic and systematic change happened. Instead of being a church looking for a silver bullet, develop and follow microsteps to achieve your turnaround dreams. Let me define microsteps as I am using them here. Microsteps are a series of small steps taken to move the church forward over time, seen through deliberate actions to pause, plan, and promote the future.

Pause Before Embarking on a Change

When the church is declining and the people are desperate, they will do one of two things that are polar opposites. One group will hunker down and want to keep everything the same, hoping that by waiting things will change on their own. The second group will want to change things drastically and create even more upheaval within the church. Instead of doing nothing, or doing too much, the microstep of pausing is a crucial element in helping people recognize the need to adapt to the current situation the church finds itself in. To move from decline into a space of renewal, pausing to evaluate the current landscape within the church is essential. Arianna Huffington wrote, "The benefit of even one small win goes beyond just the new healthy behavior you've created—it actually builds that willpower muscle to create even more wins and good habits."[3] See these pauses as reflective microsteps that help the church find a new way forward by reflecting on the past and present.

Observing through listening is a win, as you glean information from others' concerns and ideas from inside and outside the church walls; a leader begins to hear how to lead. It is in the pause step that reflection can take place. Ownership of past missteps can take place and development of a new way forward from decline can begin. There may be a tendency for a leader to push past this microstep and try to overcome the challenges by moving things fast, forgetting that the legacy of missteps will not go away without acknowledging them through reflection and reviewing what went wrong.

3. Huffington, "Microsteps."

Plan Through Small Microwins

Leading change can be challenging as diverging interests push and pull their agenda in the name of the Lord. Leaders should begin to plan small wins where diverging interests can be brought together, focusing on the main interest of rebounding from decline and obeying God's will for the local community. In every church, there are small wins that, when combined, can create momentum that will move the church from the rut of discouragement to the progress of forward momentum.

Though your church might have limited resources (people, finances, and community partnerships), evaluate where it can use its limited resources to make a big move. Sometimes, this takes moving resources from one area to another to make sure that the new initiative progresses forward. Plan to develop several early wins that will build on each other to create the needed momentum to push more considerable changes that must take place in the future. Developing microwins that everyone can celebrate will generate an atmosphere of excitement that will help the leader and the congregation navigate the change that will come next. Through strategic planning and implementation of initiatives, small microwins will help the church look past failures and celebrate future successes.

Promote Success Through Microstories

The story the church has been telling itself in decline has to change if it will rebound. Every person in the church is a storyteller who expresses emotional sentiments about where they think the church is going. The long-term negative sentiments will change over time through small microsteps of stories of lives transformed, children impacted through ministry, and community members engaged through a renewed purpose from the church.

The story you tell yourself as a leader is as important as the story you tell others when you speak directly to them. There may be discouraging days and seasons in ministry, but remember, God has not forgotten or forsaken the local church. Push through these doubt moments by leaning on God to guide you, as you share through your fear the faith you have in leaning into this new phase of the church. Spirit-led storytelling enables others to witness the move of God and encourages them to share the good things God is up to. Transformational leadership and change start through microstorytelling that increases the likelihood of changing the culture of the church from a negative mindset to a positive one.

Microsteps are an essential ingredient to a turnaround that will help the church move forward through pausing, planning, and promoting the new God-culture the church desperately needs, as it moves on from a negative spiritual mindset into the new frontier of renewal.

Chapter 6

Dreaming Through the Difficulty

EVERY CHURCH HAS A dream buried inside the empty rooms or hallways that connect buildings on the property together. Most established churches have seen years, maybe even decades, of numerical and financial decline. With the onset of decline, the spirit of the people shifted from serving others to saving themselves. "The reality is that when a restart becomes necessary it is because the church that died had long ago ceased to be transformational in its message and the community has suffered spiritually as a result."[1] Somewhere along the way, the members' dreams slowly became snuffed out by the reality of the treasurer's report or number-board that counted attendance hanging on the wall. The promise of what was became captured by what reality is today, and instead of faith, fear set in.

If you have served in church leadership for a short period or a long tenure, it is never too late to begin to dream again through the difficulty that the church has gone through in the past. Whatever your local church is facing today is never a reason to stop dreaming and believing that God can do it again and help grow the church. For many in the church today, the spirit of defeatism has taken hold and must be set aside to honor God's call on the local church and begin to move forward.

1. Cheyney and Sells, *Life After Death*, 21.

Dream What Could Be

The church God has called you to is remarkable. He has a purpose and a promise to deliver through your ministry if you are willing to help the church dream what could be. Instead of fretting about what the church does not have or what has been lost, see what God sees—empty classrooms to be used as space for programs the community needs. A space creatively repurposed to meet the community's future needs and to capture a new way of reaching the community by focusing not only on Sunday mornings but every day of the week.

The average church is underutilizing its property and struggles to fill it on a typical day. Why not dream beyond Sunday mornings and Wednesday nights and see what more can be done through buildings, unused space, and property? Begin to dream of partnerships by laying the ground beforehand through agreeing as church members on which space, rooms, or portions of the property can be used for God-ministry opportunities, even before you have an agreement from a partner. Having the church leadership, board, and members in agreement before you launch a God-partnership will lessen any misunderstandings in the future.

God has incredible plans for your local church, but the people must get out of God's way and allow God to move.

Dream What Is

After years of decline, your facility might have a lot of deferred maintenance. That is nothing new for a pastoral leader who can see past the worn-out carpets, outdated bathrooms, or the parking lot that looks more like a grass meadow than a place to park cars. However, guests cannot or will not get over an unsightly place. If your local church wants to move from the difficult and into the dream stage, then as a leader you must begin to trust God with what you have. I have found as a revitalization specialist that many local churches do not have a plan to reignite the God-vision that seemingly vanished from the church grounds. They want to blame former pastors, members, or even the community they want to reach. STOP IT! Stop blaming others for the problems. The problems are here. Realize that no one can go back and change the past, so stop it and find a way to move forward.

The church must begin to dream of what is by facing the reality of where they find themselves. If the people or leadership's viewpoint does not change, no amount of blessing from God will turn the church around unless they fully surrender to God's will. See the deferred maintenance challenges as God-opportunities to seek wise counsel from others and God in order to move forward. Do not allow the fear of a dollar sign to overcome God's plan he has placed inside of you. Begin to dream again by taking on each project individually, ranking them, and chipping away at them. There may be a tendency to be overwhelmed by all that needs to be accomplished; know that the church did not decline overnight and will not be restored overnight, but through consistency things will begin to look up.

Dream What Will Be

As the church has declined, many who remained became quite negative and harmful in assessing buildings, programs, and leaders who have led through the decline. Through their words and actions, they have forestalled any forward progress as they keep building walls where God wants to build a bridge to the dream he has for them. Instead of being caught up in what happened in the past, shift your words to harbor a future outlook of hope and destiny within a turnaround. Dream of what will be in the future by projecting a forward-looking outlook that sees past the limitations and turns them over to the limitless God.

Without having a dream of where you want to lead the church, the people will not follow. Without a positive story told through sermons, personal conversations, small group gatherings, and social media posts, the negative will destroy what God can do in the church. God did not make a mistake when he called the leadership of the church you serve today. If God calls you, you must be obedient in helping the people dream of what will be. It will take intentional conversations, prayer times with members, vision casting, vision retelling when people forget, and a positive God-honoring spirit when the adversary uses good people to throw up roadblocks to stop progress. Do not allow the past to dictate your church's future. Free yourself by dreaming of what can be as you work together to accomplish God's plans.

While you may be facing a difficult season, do not allow dreams to die because the church is underwhelmed by people and overwhelmed by problems. Begin to dream again, and let God guide the church through this difficult season into a season of promise.

DEALING WITH REBELLIOUS PEOPLE

Listening to a pastor friend recently, I could hear the pain in his voice as he found out one of his staff members was speaking about him behind his back to key leaders in the church. He had come to a place of either defending his reputation and leadership or ignoring the problem, hoping it would go away. The pain he felt has been touched by many who have served in leadership dating back to Moses' time. In Num 14:1–9, Moses and Aaron are faced with an uprising over their decision to conquer the land God had given them. While many raised the white flag to give in to the temptation of staying put, Joshua and Caleb, two of the original twelve spies, tore their garments (Num 14:6) and cried out to God.

How many times as a leader have you found yourself dealing with an uprising from an influential select few because they disagreed with where God had asked you to take them? But for Israel, the difference would cost the whole community forty years and most people's lives because they chose to disobey God and honor their selfish wishes. Within a few lines of Scripture (Num 14:5–9), God reveals five ways to deal with rebellious people that are still valid for today's church.

Repent of Past Sins

Once the rebellion had taken hold, the camp leaders were shocked that the people would turn on them and God so quickly. That pain has been felt countless times by ministers who have led people and churches from one season into another. They were leading like Christ, only to fall prey to the vile efforts of humankind. The valuable lesson that Moses and others showed was to repent of their sins and cry out to God to redeem them from the sinful nature of the community to which they belonged. As a leader, you cannot control how others act or what they will say, but you can acknowledge to God in a time of prayer and fasting the sin in the camp and repent of those sins as well as your own.

Repair Unholy Damage

As the rebellion was widespread, the leaders quickly reminded the community how God had shown up and blessed before; yet no amount of remembering could change the hardened hearts of those who took on fear over faith. The leaders did their best to rally the troops by reminding the wayward members of God's promises and past victories, but to no avail. The spiritual die had been cast and harmed the community's future. Through remembrance, a leader can provide a pivot point of healing as an off-ramp of rebellion, but the rebellious ones must accept or deny it. Sadly, many churches are being closed or split because of the revolutionary nature of unrepentance among leaders and members alike. God wants to see a restoration of the church through acknowledgment of past wrongs, a repented heart, and a willingness to find a new way forward.

Remove Idols Holding You Back

Every church I have served and every member I have met has had to deal with idols as they obey what God has called them to do, including me. Idols are strongholds that hold back God's will for the church or persons because of personal preference. The Israelite leaders realized rather quickly that the faith community had turned to a community of fear, which was driving their decision-making, and that they had to do something quick, or the promised land would slip away.

The Lord shone in the tent as the people grumbled and considered stoning Moses and the others. As God entered the meeting, the community was at a spiritual fork in the road where they could obey or cling to personal idols. They chose the latter and would be struck by death, disease, and destruction. God does not want a program but a pattern of obedience that shows complete surrender. Be a leader who surrenders their ministry and mission in the local church to God.

Recover Through Obedience

If there is a chance to recover and return to God, then you must try to find a way. Recovering from sinful wants is obedience by turning from sin and returning to the Lord, but sadly churches are turning to their desires under the guise of God's will. The Israelites lost the promise because they wanted it their way and not God's. Serving the wishes of the Lord should be easy, but it's difficult for many because they allow their desires to take hold. Even Moses, their leader, would miss out on the promised land, and I wonder how many pastors miss out on God's best because they have found themselves in the community's camp and not God's.

Recovery will not be painless because there is accountability for past actions, but in the end it will restore the relationship lost in the interval and prepare the future to honor God in acts and deeds.

Receive the Promised Land

I bet you have been where Moses was: confronted by a rebellious spirit, targeted by character assassination, and maligned by innuendos all because you dared to honor God in a revitalization effort.

Moses acted out of compassion for his people and obedience to God's call on his ministry. While the people abandoned God, Moses leaned into a relationship with him. Though he did not enter the promised land, God rewarded him in the continuance of walking with him until his final days. Sometimes the promised land is not a place or time but a space with God. This book is a testament to the fact that revitalization is complex. For some members, it was easier to walk away from the church, mock me as the pastor, or lambast me for perceived slights or actions. Staff members sabotaged my work and relationships inside the church and fed into the culture of toxicity that came to light from past sins of the church. Through it all, God provided a feeling of peace in my spirit, a steel spine to the church board, and a focus to pray for everyone, even the ones who were hurting the church.

You may be leading a rebellious people, much like Moses. You can either obey God or surrender to the sinful nature by lashing out and fighting with others inside the church. The choice is ultimately yours. The promise of God is still valid for you and your local church. "Send some men to explore the land. . .which I am giving" (Num 13:2). God does not want you to give in to the rebellion but to rely on him for help moving forward into the future.

LEADING THROUGH ADVERSITY

Change is never easy, but when it comes to an institution such as the church, it can be hard to shift from how things always have been done to doing them anew. Many leaders resist the temptation to change because they fear the consequences of change. Change in a church can lead to members leaving, tithes withheld, disgruntled comments shared publicly and privately, negative social media posts, and outright warfare between the pastor and a layperson in the church. Suppose you have been in leadership for some time. In that case, you have faced the headwinds of negativity that can cause burnout, stress, and anxiety, which leads to many pastors walking away from ministry or at least their current ministry assignment. Instead of the leader giving into the temptation to give up, what if God can use the adverse circumstances to help strengthen the spiritual fortitude of the pastor and church? Revitalization is challenging in the best of circumstances. Add in stress, expectations, and people's perceived desires and you might as well give up. But you must remember that in the weeks when disappointment is plenty, God has called you to this work. God has called you to the church. And God can restore what the enemy has stolen.

Pray Your Spiritual Guts Out

While pastoring in Louisville, Kentucky, in 2016, I invited Kevin McDonald and Jeremiah Wood to help the church rethink how we served the local community. In one of the sessions, they spoke about "praying your spiritual guts out." That phrase has stuck with me all these many years later. In a world constantly calling into question the motives of leaders, it is no wonder that the authority of the pastor's office has been maligned by those who disagree with the leader. Disagreements in years past would have been kept inside the church, but with the advent of social media, negative feelings spread like wildfire, exposing a broader audience. While leaders cannot control what others say, they can control how they react.

The battle for the heart and soul of the local church is one against darkness and principalities and cannot be conquered through personalities but through prayer. Prayer must be the driving force behind everything accomplished inside the local church. Every meeting, conversation, and interaction should be bathed in prayer, as the evil one will use any opening to widen the gap between disagreeing partners. Do not fall prey to a lack of praying, but pray as if your spiritual life depends on it because it does. In the early morning hours, I enjoy walking around the campus just thinking and talking with God. With nearly fifty thousand square feet under the roof, there is a lot of space to walk and be alone with God. In these early morning walks with God, he re-centers my spirit to dig in for what is about to come during the day. Some days it's easy, and others make you want to walk away. But through it all, God restores my soul and strengthens my spirit to keep going.

Looking back on some tough days during my first year, there were times when you could have cut the tension between staff members and myself in the church office. Either way, it was uncomfortable, but as the truth was exposed and tough decisions were made for the overall long-term health of the church, the devil fought back, using good people to say and do hurtful things. I share this painful experience with you because I want you to know, dear reader, that the work is hard, but God will see you and the church through it.

Prepare as if the Ministry Depends on It

As a leader, people will look to you for direction and insight on how to move forward. If you overact positively or negatively, it will sway how others react. As you analyze a situation, see the problem from all sides, seek counsel, and move forward only when you know God is in it. You can do much in your power, but when you are battling adversity, your giftings will not be enough to overcome the problem. God must be the anchor and the lens that you hold fast to as you view the situation through his eyes. While you do not have to be the most intelligent person in the room, be the most open to hearing arguments from both sides, process what each person is saying, value the words shared even if you disagree with them, find commonality amid the confusion, and lead the conversation to a conclusion. Thinking is so underrated. As the pressure grows on the changes afoot in the church, you will need more time to reflect and think. Find time to think. Spending time to think restores the soul and enables you to react accordingly to what is happening. In the most pressure-filled time, I would walk around the property, thinking and clearing my head by processing what was happening, which allowed me to find out what God wanted and ways to enact his plan over man's plan for the local church.

In moving a church from decline to rebound, many hurdles have to be tackled, and as a leader you must know what you do not know and be humble enough to allow stronger voices to speak into the process. It is then that, as a leader, you can help guide the process to a conclusion that honors all sides. Do not be afraid of not having all the answers, but be frightened if you think you do. Be willing to listen to opposing views and decipher the other person's feelings and what is meaningful to the discussion to move the situation forward. It will take discernment and removing ego, on the leader's part, to hear opposing views in a bid to move forward into the future together. The focus should not be your view of winning but God's view taking shape. The trouble is that many want to win instead of surrendering to God's divine plans.

Partner with Others, and Never Serve Alone

Partnering in ministry can be twofold, as seen through Jesus' example of discipleship and dependency. Since the beginning of time, God saw that humans need a helper to work alongside. So too, in the local church, the pastoral leader cannot lead alone. The church leadership team (board, elders, deacons, influential members) should be a diverse group of people that support the forward momentum of the church. The pastor should give them permission to speak into the decision-making in a way that respects the pastor and provides clarity through insight that the pastor might not see.

As a leader, do not isolate yourself from the general congregation, but be proactive in inviting people who can speak truth to power to help you delineate if you are on the right or wrong path. Jesus taught his converts through large and small group discipleship models. He encouraged them to ask questions and allowed them to learn from their mistakes. Even though he could have handled all the problems alone, he constantly sought God's counsel in prayer. As a leader, model the Jesus behavior you want others to gain. If a leader is not reading the word on Sunday mornings, the people will not see the value in the word during the week. If a leader is not praying like Jesus, do not expect your people to pray regularly. Leading is knowing that others are watching. Discipleship and dependency principles were not just for Jesus' day but today. These foundational principles can help a leader lead through adversity and come out the other side better for it.

Participate with God to Be Jesus to Others

The hardest part of adversity is still loving the person you disagree with. You would think that in the church everyone would get along, but change something and watch the reactions that come forth. Each person who enters the church weekly brings a lifetime of experiences that have shaped their reaction to how things should be handled. Instead of placing your way of handling things on someone, lean into the conversation and listen for cues to help you find a middle ground to build a foundation to move forward. Disagreements happen in all facets of life, but instead of giving in to the temptation of placing blame, find a way forward by being Jesus to the other person. Let me pause you here. Hard conversations should be okay inside the church. However, some have lost their church by having conversations with a power faction in the church.

Jesus' example in Scripture showed he was a man of compassion, conviction, and care. He led with a heart of love, stayed firm to biblical principles, and cared for the person he interacted with. Adversity advertises that the church is moving forward and that the devil wants to distract the church and its leadership. Do not be caught fighting with church members; be seen fighting the evil one through prayer and positive conversation.

HONORING GOD WHEN HURT BY THE CHURCH

When people leave the church, as a leader it can feel personal, and sometimes it is personally directed at the leader. What should you do if you find yourself in a position where a key leader has left the church and laid the blame at your feet? Every member who has left the church has pained me. It is not easy losing a member of the family, but what do you do? You can flee, fight, or reconfigure your leadership. The choice will be yours. For me, I chose to fight (stand my ground) for the church.

Flee from the Turmoil to Find Peace in a New Place

Many who leave the church do so hoping to get away from the turmoil in the place where they used to find rest. However, they soon find peace will only come if they have addressed the underlying cause of the fallout. In a world fraught with disagreements, the church should be a place where they are resolved using biblical principles found throughout Scripture. Worldly ways have seeped into the church, and disputes are handled much like in the marketplace, which leaves all sides embittered. Through lies and innuendos, opportunities to resolve the conflict through conversation, confession, and Christ-love are missed, and the church must grieve God in how it has acted.

Instead of fleeing, what if those who disagreed could set aside personal feelings and lean into the God-calling on their lives? Could God show up in a time of repentance and of retreat from worldly ways? I imagine so, and through the tough, heart-filled conversations, Christ-centered love could begin to repair the broken relationship to keep the person in the church or at least enable them to leave the church with a more open heart to its leadership team. Fleeing may not be the answer, but falling on one's knees in open repentance to God for their part in the disagreement enables healing to begin in one's heart.

Fight for Position and Power in the Face of Pushback

I heard it once from a long-term church member, "I was here before you came, and I will be here long after you leave." The sentiments directed at me were apparent and immediate. God, in that instance, was relegated to the passenger seat while the member drove the spiritual direction of the church. Power plays between members and pastors are played countless times in churches weekly, with spiritually deadly consequences. The local church has two clear leadership models: lay-led and staff-led leadership. When these two leadership ideas clash, the church becomes bruised and battered. Who wins? No one!

The power in the church does not lie in the pastor or the layperson but in Christ. The word of God has more power in a chapter of the Bible than a leader has in one sentence of a conversation. Why? Because God is the one in control of the local church. If the power equation is out of sync with biblical principles, then the pastor and church members must find a way back from their power grab and re-center their spirits back on why the church exists in the first place. The church is meant to glorify God, and that includes in words as much as actions and deeds. Through prayer, biblical direction, and obedience to God, the relationship between the pastor and lay leader can be restored if both sides surrender their will for God's will.

Reconfigure Your Leadership to Meet Current and Future Needs in the Church

In every walk of life, there are times of disagreement. In the workplace, you can leave work and go home. On the other hand, you can go to work and flee home if there are disagreeable times. But in the spiritual realm, it affects every aspect of your life. The relationship between a person and God is sacred. When members of the same church or denomination clash over their interpretation of Scripture and guidance, they banish God and harm their witness as a church to the general population. We see this played out on social media daily, where Christians attack each other and harm those watching from their devices. There were times people shared hurtful outright lies about my ministry to others, who knew better, inside the church or just after they left. I never confronted the maligning of my leadership. I simply prayed. Prayer is so simple at the outset, but it restores the soul. Through prayer I chose not to allow the insults to dictate my response back to them. Instead, I focused on the calling. God is calling the local church and its leaders to reconfigure their preferences for a leadership continuum that challenges the status quo and elevates humility above personalities.

As the church revitalizer faces forces against their leadership calling, they must either elevate the problem or their leadership.

The desire of any leader should be to lower the conflict by honoring the calling in their life, supporting others, and developing a team of lay leaders who have an outward focus to reach the lost with the gospel of Christ. The goal of a leader should not be to win an argument but to win souls. It will take a leadership configuration, a mind shift especially, to see that every disagreement is not a fight and that faith in the system is as essential as faith in following God. You may have found this chapter more challenging because it forced you to think through past hurt. But without working through the hurt, you cannot fully heal. The same is true for a local church. Without reviewing the past, you will not be able to allow Christ to guide you through the healing process that comes after a season of crises in the church or your life.

Chapter 7

Future-Forward Budgeting

As you do the work, you will reach a point where the next steps must be made. These are challenging steps. They will be painful because they will lead to difficult decisions. However, these are necessary steps to move the church forward into a season of church health. The budget will be one area of major review and will drive the priorities from the idea lab. The church leadership team should review previous quarterly and yearly budgets, comparing what came in the year before and what the leadership team projects will come in within the following year. A word of caution: be conservative with these numbers. You would rather have a surplus than a negative amount at the end of the budget cycle. "We don't give to get; we give to obey. We let God deal with the aftermath in the way He chooses."[1] Yes, faith is good, but common sense also comes into play.

Let me pause you here; if your church does not operate with a formulated budget that spells out where funds are allocated through line items, then you are setting yourself back. Let me explain: the budget is like a roadmap that helps guide the future from point A to point B. Without a clear map, church leadership will lose its focus and find itself stuck in an area it never intended to go.

---

1. Betzer, *Some Churches Are Blessed*.

These check-in times enable the leaders to reflect on the organization's mission and how best to use the church's finite resources through leadership conversations and data-driven decision-making from the financial and numerical numbers collected throughout the month through services, accounts, and payroll liabilities. The check-ins will help the team pivot when challenges come.

Let me encourage you to start leading your team through future-forward budgeting with the idea of planning now for the future. There are three areas I would encourage any church to consider when reviewing the budget framework:

1. Reinvest in the church's infrastructure to prepare for future activities and guests.
2. Repair community relationships through connections.
3. Restore the focus from self to the Savior.

The uncomfortable truth is that leaders want to stay comfortable, so they keep the status quo even if it will hurt them two or three years down the road. Future-forward budgeting forces tough conversations not driven by personalities or desires but through data-driven decision-making, which comes directly from the numbers.

Reinvest in the Church's Infrastructure to Prepare for Future Activities and Guests

As you lean into future-forward budget decision-making, the challenge is to help lead your leadership team to see past current needs and address the ministry's future. Take microsteps to develop a community culture that sees past the four walls of the church building and sees the building as people advancing the kingdom of God. In this way, you face the uncomfortable truths in reviewing each budget line item, position, and program related to that line item. By moving from being comfortable in conformity, you help the church move toward advancing the church into the future.

This stage means cutting away at people's preferences to advance a future life for the church by allowing data to drive decision-making, which removes preferences and emotions from the equation. There is a saying that "numbers do not lie." In the case of the church, we often ignore the numbers to the detriment of the overall health of the church because we insert our likes and dislikes into the equation. By using future-forward budgeting, the church leadership enables the church to begin to create space for development that focuses on a culture of community connection that bridges the pew with connecting to people outside the church's walls. This process is painful because it forces everyone to face the current realities others may want to ignore, but it is necessary in helping the church progress forward and reach its God-potential.

Our church budget evaluation process was thorough and comprehensive, leaving no stone unturned. We came to understand that every member or leader supports evaluating the budget until you propose reducing their area of ministry or area of support. The reality is that numbers don't lie, and the evaluated numbers, as seen through bills, payroll, offering, overall giving, etc., will tell the story of what you must do to turn around the dying church. We had taken months to establish a budget, allowing diverse voices to speak into the process. I am not recommending this process, but this is the process we took, and it worked for us. Three members of the church's seven-member finance committee met over ten times to review every line item in the budget and make recommendations to the entire finance committee. I became part of the process when they had reviewed and agreed on at least 75 percent of the budget. It was clear the one area they could only solve with my input was staffing levels. A year before I arrived, the jurisdictional leader, whom we call a district superintendent, had told the church board that they needed to cut the staffing line item to no more than 48 percent of the budget. At the time, it was nearly 60 percent of the budget. The previous church board made some cuts (cutting a youth pastor and other line items) but did not approach the figure the superintendent had recommended.

Instead of kicking the financial can down the road, I was determined to fix the budget in one fell swoop. It would be painful, but it would stop the death by a thousand cuts that the last thirteen years had brought about. Swift action would be the reaction of the day. Meeting with the budget committee, they voted two-to-one to recommend deep staffing cuts to rebalance the budget and meet the district leader's recommendation from the previous year. Next up, the full finance committee reviewed the information, and the early nonformal vote was four-to-three against the cuts. It was not a way to build consensus, but the consensus was what we needed to enact sweeping cuts to the budget and overall staffing while maintaining support from church members. After a very emotional and frank second meeting, the finance committee voted to recommend the cuts with six votes for the new budget and one abstention. Next up, the church board would review the draft budget.

When the church board reviewed the recommendations, it went over like a lead balloon. There was a clear division, shock, and a realization for many that revitalization would be painful. My goal was for the church board to review, talk, and above all pray together three times over a month as the deadline to enact a new budget was approaching. According to our church manual, if any staffing cuts are made, the church must provide thirty-day notice if it's less than six weeks from the end of our church year. Either way, this issue was coming to a head. No decision was made at the first meeting. The board chose to move up the second meeting. Entering the meeting, it was clear from what board members had shared with me beforehand that three members would support the budget and six would not, thus freezing the current staffing levels in place. In my mind, this would cripple the church, delay the inevitable, and would speed the church closer to death. Right before the meeting, I went to the restroom, washed my face, and said, "Okay, Lord, you called me here." Instead of being negative, I promised God to be the happy warrior, but I knew in my heart we would be doomed if we kept things the same.

After an hour of earnest deliberation, I asked for a vote from the board. I asked each member around the table to share their vote and their thought process one by one. With one member remaining, the vote was four-to-four. As the final board member shared their reasoning for voting for the budget, thus staffing cuts,

I let out an audible gasp at the five-to-four vote in favor of the new budget. In the final vote, God had given me his answer to my prayerful cry just an hour before.

I was still unsettled, maybe because of the emotional hour or because I sensed God wanting more from us. As a pastor or leader in the church, the responsibility of making decisions that align with the church's values and mission is paramount. Over the ensuing hours, the board found a way to become unified and revoted, with the board voting unanimously for the budget. This action would prove to the lay members of the church that the action was not taken lightly but with God's guidance. It would cut staffing levels to under 40 percent of the budget and would carry forward swift changes to the church.

The announcement was made to the congregation the following Sunday, as the staff had been alerted a few days before. It was a very difficult decision, but it was the right one for the church's future. The next step was whether the church provided a severance. The board chose to pay out all vacation owed to the employees up to their last day of employment, three months of salary, along with benefits such as health insurance and retirement. In total the church would pay fifty-six thousand dollars to help the employees adjust to the new realities as the church entered uncharted territory. Even though the church was very generous in providing severance, some church members and former staff felt the church could have done more. I will let others judge if the act was generous or not. All I know for certain was the turnaround was extremely painful for all who participated.

With the budget cut, seventeen people would walk out the door in the next three months, including the four now-former staff members. One member who left was a board member who voted for the budget but whose spouse could not support the church any longer. Looking back, it was the hardest decision for everyone involved to make, but it was the right one for the church's situation. With the cuts, the budget reallocated dollars that were allocated to go to the staffing line item and redirected the funds into a backlog of infrastructure needs. Five new air conditioners, an updated elevator, new wiring for our compassionate ministries building, wiring for our community center, and several electrical panel boxes were upgraded within the first eight months of the new church year, not counting the transformation that took place in our former gym. More on that story in the final chapters.

Repair Community Relationships Through Connections

As the church declined over the years, it had spent increasing resources propping up programs and staff positions that no longer met its current needs. With the decline of tithes, the leadership pooled its resources inward, and fewer funds were spent attracting or reaching outside the walls. The church, which used to be well-known in the community, became increasingly unknown, triggering a more profound dependence on its current limited resources. This in turn forces the leadership not to invest in potential outreach, feeding into the cycle of decline. This is where we found ourselves when I took over. We were looking inward, rearranging the deck chairs of the titanic (our local church) as we were sinking. Without major action we were going to close our doors. Maybe not overnight but within a few years. As we began to adapt and change, some fought the change with words, by withholding tithes, or by leaving the church.

Developing lasting partnerships that impact the community might show little success in the pew through numerical growth at Sunday services, but stay with it, for the church must ask, "Why has God placed us here in this neighborhood? To reach 'us' or 'others'?" The focus should not be on pew sitters alone but on serving others to win them to the gospel. With an investment in the community, the church invests in a community-center model that implores us to impact a more significant swath of the community and revitalizes the church through multiple volunteer opportunities, prayer partnerships, and community connections. For a stagnant and dying church, new life brings new hope and will someday return the investment made to the community with new Christians that will become part of the local church. This process is long, and it must be understood that there is no quick return on investment. Remember how long the church has been uninvested in the community. It might take double that time to return a new investment in the resources that you spend. Be patient and allow God to lead as you serve. Fruit will come only if you keep sowing your time, talent, and treasure into those around you by committing to prayer, fasting, and loving others.

Restore the Focus from Self to the Savior

As you help your team lean into future-forward budgeting, direct your leadership to begin to see past self-wants and return their heart and desires to what God wants the local church to accomplish. This focus from self to Savior seems easy, but it is a fight between the flesh, which leans into preferences over God's power, and the Holy Spirit, which is called to guide the local church. Help members to stop focusing on their needs and shift resources to focus on the needs of others. This one act will be painful for those in the pew to process and may cause an exodus of people in the short term until the reality of what is taking place is of God and not driven by man's desires or personalities. Hold firm. Do the work today, and trust God for tomorrow. Ignore the nay sayers and demoralizers, and focus on the calling to win the lost.

Realize as the church declined in the past, the remnant who remained held tightly to those who held the semblance of leadership because it provided safety in the ever-changing landscape of decline. However, that false sense of security creates a win-lose proposition because when changes have to be made, the people will feel betrayed by their safety net. The reality is that change comes to even those who hide from it, and by taking a proactive response to evaluate all current and future needs as part of the budget process, the church brings to light areas that need to be sunset and other areas that need new life. The power of the Savior must become paramount over the will of those in leadership in order to see where he is guiding and to follow through by walking in his steps.

Evaluate the needs as you seek God's plan for the future, and watch how he restores the crestfallen church into a community-centered church by budgeting with a future-forward leadership posture.

DO NOT WAIT TO TACKLE DEFERRED MAINTENANCE IN THE CHURCH

The American church has a problem. It is aging. Not only is the attendance of members aging but so are its buildings. Any revitalizer who has gone to a church faces the obstacle of deferred maintenance. With an aging population and facilities, the one-two punch of deferred maintenance is killing the church. So, what should a church leadership team do if they find themselves in a situation where the deferred maintenance issues are swallowing up the church's budget? The easy answer would be to run. I know I almost did that very first week. In all reality, God did not plant the church or call you to lead it just to run from the responsibility of turning around a struggling church.

I want to share four critical areas for evaluating the next steps as you begin to tackle deferred maintenance issues inside the church.

Review the Facility from an Inspector's Perspective

When a church deals with deferred maintenance, the church must not move towards patch-up jobs done with too little money or expertise. It should begin investing in the long-term viability of the buildings and ministry on the grounds. Many churches find themselves where they are today because the church set about solving matters with in-house expertise that, at times, did not have the resources or understanding of how to solve the problem for the long term. The patchwork of maintenance inevitably delays the real fix to the problem that must be dealt with today.

If you do not know what to do, bring in a general contractor or even a real estate inspector to review the facility and provide an overview of suggestions that the church board can review with real-time costs. If not, you could cost the church more money in the long term. The assessment will help get the board to review the same data points simultaneously, rather than what they might feel should be done. By taking out feelings and focusing on facts, the board can devise a plan of action to help the church begin to tackle the crises they find themselves in.

Develop a Plan to Begin to Solve the Problems

Once the church knows what they are facing, the leadership team needs to rank the needs from critical to commonplace, with the major issues being dealt with immediately. The vital problems found in the inspection of the building might be hidden from most of the church. As it is, a lot of behind-the-wall issues, such as wiring or a new roof, will take all the leadership to speak about why the needs must be addressed and how it will help the church in the long term. As the church team begins to lay forth a plan, that plan should be incremental as it assists the church in progressing forward one project at a time. It will take tactical patience and foresight for a church revitalizer to see the larger picture when others only see the project or the momentous challenges before them.

As the leadership ranks each item and begins championing the plan, now there will be those questioning why one project is starting before another. Your role will be to explain the "why" behind the "what," and proclaim the project's value. Help others see the value, not in work but in the investment to see lives changed through the church of the future. Reclaim the plan if it gets off track by lay leaders by keeping the message of the "why" and "what" all about God.

Stay Focused and Do Not Chase the Fire

As the maintenance projects from the list begin to see completion, other unanswered questions or projects will come to view. Well-intentioned people will try to pull the vision away from the project list and the rank order toward what most people are talking about. This mission creep will destroy any positive momentum and derail future plans. I encourage you to stay focused. Do not allow the fire (the loudest voices) to get in the way of God's plan for the local church. Sadly, too many churches fail, not because they do not have a plan but because they fail to work it.

There will always be projects that could take the number one spot on the work order list. When *you* work the plan, not the *plan* working the church, the project list will be completed. The people will see the results and be willing to invest in future projects. Staying calm in the fire and directing the team (board or members) to maintain the course while you field the church's concerns will enable the church to see better days through a solid structural and financial footing. Your goal as a leader should be to put out the fires and not help spread them.

Review Where You Can Cut to Invest

With the project list developed and the ranking of what projects will go first, the issue of "how do we pay for these projects?" will come up in conversation. As a leader, you must help the church board see the broader picture by walking them through the current realities of where the church finds itself. At this stage, they must know the cost of deferred maintenance, the cost of repairs, and where the church finds themselves financially. This stage is the death stage. The people must die to the image of who they thought the church was and where it is today in order to rise in Christ-vision for the church. The budget has to be updated with adjustments to prepare to increase ministry in the future. Painful cuts might have to be made to staffing, programs, or other ministries so the church can invest in the future by fixing deferred maintenance issues.

By evaluating today, you create a new opportunity to minister in a new way tomorrow. Once the church board or leadership team backs this plan, this must be explained over and over again to church members as the shock wave of change reverberates. This is not an easy stage because some members will leave, and others will disagree loudly at the differences they have with the plan; but hold steady as you help the church rightsize from the deferred maintenance nightmare, and watch how God restores what could have closed the church.

Deferred maintenance does not have to kill the church if the leadership is willing to address the issues head-on by reviewing the facility with fresh eyes, developing a plan of action, staying focused during the process, and investing in the future.

RENOVATE BY INNOVATING

Renovation and innovating became buzzwords for the first year of our turnaround. The goal was to prepare for future guests. There has been no area within the now ninety-three-year-old church that conversations and project development have not touched. Some members became negative that too much attention was being placed on the physical footprint of a church and not on current members. I, for one, have seen the renewed excitement that comes with a potential renovation mindset for the super majority of members focused on redeveloping the church to reach the community.

If you are a pastor or lay leader, you are called to serve with a vision of the future and invest through discipling members. Innovation indicates that a church's physical attributes and overall thinking are changing, leading to successful opportunities to reach more people with the gospel of Christ.

Innovate to Lead the Church Forward

As you begin to renovate the church (programs, people, and positions), you must decide the following: Who is your target audience? Where will you invest (time, talent, and treasure)? Who are you trying to reach (people group, neighborhood, or demographic)? If you know the "why" behind the "what," you will be able to hone in on your target audience.

Once you know where you want the church to begin moving, others will have to evaluate what is working (programs, style of worship, and resources that need investing). Begin discarding broken strategies, fixing what needs mending, and starting what needs to be started. This process is exciting yet challenging, as many voices will try to speak into the process. It will take a seasoned leader to navigate through the voices to find God's voice. Innovation takes creativity to see what the church could be in the future, through the church's resources, and to see the church move forward.

Innovate to Reach New People

If your local church has remained stagnant or declined over the last decade, renovating by innovating to reach new people is essential and not impossible. The first question the church must ask is, Are we willing to change? Think about it this way: Where can the need in our neighborhood or community be answered through a partnership with our local church? Your local church is strategically located to meet the needs of the people in the shadow of your church's steeple. The transformation will come if the church (its people) is willing to find the need, develop a partnership with a community agency or neighborhood association, and/or develop a strategy to meet it by investing in others.

It sounds so simple, but it will take grit to overcome self-doubt and strategic decline in order to push forward with an innovative spirit to reach the community and bless them as the hands and feet of Christ.

Innovate to Capture God's Direction

Leading change is not just a physical attribute but a spiritual one. It is easy to transform a space. Through the work of the Holy Spirit and scriptural teaching, the community will begin to know that the church cares. In return the community will begin to care about the church. God has an incredible plan for the local church, but it must trust him by embracing his plan, process, and partnership that he helps provide. The church must not only pray but also participate: participate with God in doing its part, preparing the facility, and preparing missional workers who will serve others around them.

The local church's leadership should ask themselves, What is God asking us to do? What are we willing to do as part of the process? What steps need to be taken over the next week, month, quarter, and year to achieve meaningful connection with our neighbors and future guests? Following God's direction is about innovating and adapting to the needs found throughout the process. Trust me, God will restore the church by restoring its focus to others if the members' hearts are geared toward what God wants.

Renovating by innovating is dreaming new dreams, being intentional about planning but also executing the plan. The sentiment of "build it and they will come," must become "go and tell" the story of how Jesus helped lives transform by serving others without expecting anything in return. God will restore what the locust has stolen, and the community of believers will be better for it if the church is willing to submit to his authority.

USING TECHNOLOGY TO COMMUNICATE COMMUNITY INSIDE THE CHURCH WORKS

With change comes the need for the church to adapt to the changing times by helping members stay connected. Sure, every church wants to grow and gain new members. That is the calling outlined in the Great Commission (Matt 28:16–20) by Jesus. But with the Church aging and shrinking, as we were, we needed to permit ourselves to invest in current members at the same time we were preparing for guests. There were five practical ways in which the church saw transformation from Sunday gatherings only into fellowship that extends into the week.

The average worship attendee is well into their "baby boom" years and has had to learn to adapt over their lifetime. As their families have moved away, and the neighborhood changed, the one thing that stayed constant was the local church. With every new change, they have had to adapt to the culture outside the church and cling to the familiar relationships inside the local church. According to Pew Research, "30% of U.S. adults say they go online to search for information about religion. 21% use apps or websites to help them read the Bible or other religious scriptures. 15% listen to religion-focused podcasts. 14% use apps or websites to help or remind them to pray."[2] As their families moved from the community they stayed in, they had to adapt to new technologies to stay connected. So do not count out any age group when it comes to connecting through technology in and out of the church. To help strengthen these bonds of friendship, our church uses five connectional tools to create a deeper community that you may want to try at your local church.

1. **One Call System:** One Call is an incredible tool that enables the church to connect with members through voice, talk, text, and email. We use the system for weather or significant emergencies, prayer needs, or general announcements that need to be shared with the church before the next service time. With the system, you can single out small groups for notifications that do not need to go out to the larger church population.[3]

2. **QR Codes:** Many church members have smartphones that enable instant connection with the outside world. Through smartphones, the app developers have provided the local churches with free resources to use as instant connection points for sharing whatever message the church has. We installed QR codes on the back of pews and the worship

---

2. Nadeem, "Many Americans."
3. OnSolve, "One Call Now."

bulletin to provide easy access to give an offering or share information with a first time visitor. QR Codes are a non-threatening way to gather guests' contact information or have a person sign up for an event.[4]

3. **Monthly Newsletter:** At the beginning of every month, the office sends a newsletter highlighting stories about what has taken place in the month previous using Constant Contact to disseminate the information. While this is a paid platform, free platforms, such as MailChimp, are on the open marketplace that a church could choose from. These tools are another way to inform members and keep those unable to attend due to health-related issues feeling like they are a part of the church.

4. **Social Media Groups:** Social media can be used for either good or evil purposes. Instead of lamenting the adverse effects, begin to see it as a tool that can be harnessed to connect people inside the church. Collaboration can occur through private social media pages, and a deeper faith walk can happen outside of just a few hours a week at the church. While the heart of the church is consistently winning souls on the outside, social media can be used to strengthen a faith-giver's walk inside the church.

5. **Instant Directory:** The newest tool we have deployed is an online directory that provides the user with a pictorial guide for church members' information that they have provided. From birthdays, anniversaries, and more, this resource is a vital part of keeping folks connected through phone/text messages and personal notes that bring a familiar touch to a technology driven world.[5]

These practical tools have enhanced the existing community of fellowship and strengthened the relational bonds that come through a Christ-centered gathering.

4. For a QR code generator, see www.the-qrcode-generator.com.
5. See www.instantchurchdirectory.com.

Chapter 8

Win One for Jesus

IN 1931, A PIONEERING church planter named Viva Crawford set out from Lakeland, Florida, to plant a holiness church in Winter Haven, Florida, some thirteen miles away. While today the drive from the two city centers would take less than forty minutes, in those days the transportation system slowed any progress. The burgeoning city of just seven thousand residents positioned the new holiness church as a beacon of hope in rural central Florida. In partnership with her husband, Pastor Crawford began knocking on doors throughout the community to share, with anyone who would open their doors, about Jesus. It became apparent that this soul-winning team needed a building to call a church home. A former Methodist-turned-Catholic church in town was vacant and was a perfect spot to plant a new church. On one side of the church was a Masonic Hall, and on the other side were a series of local businesses. Pastor Crawford quickly found out that the rented building could be the church's rent-free if the new church took care of the property. According to church records, in one period of her early ministry, she made "33 pastoral calls, contacted 109 new homes, prayed in 35 homes, and received $23, eight lemons, and half dozen limes as her salary."[1] Pastor Crawford was a tena-

---

1. Winter Haven Board, "Charles Kirby."

cious caller who would visit home after home. If she found a hint of interest from a family, she would return time and time until they agreed to come to church or accept Jesus into their hearts.

Maybe she wore them down, but her calling won many families to Jesus. When you evaluate your local church, who in the church is on fire for the Lord? Who is inviting unchurched friends? That is your Pastor Crawford. That is the one who should be let loose, encouraged, and celebrated for being the John the Baptist in your midst. However, too many churches pour cold water on the on-fire member because they lack authority, education, or approval from the leaders inside the church. Sometimes, as a leader in the church, you have to get out of the way and allow the Spirit to guide. Consider this: Crawford was a Nazarene female pastor trying to start a church in the middle of a depression and seeking new converts. The Nazarene Church had only started in 1908, as a denomination branching from the Methodist Church. One of its earliest ordained elders was knocking down stereotypes and the adverse effects of planting a new church in the depression to see people accept Christ. So ask yourself, Who do you need to let go and let God move? Is it you? Are you called to win one more to the Lord?

EVERYDAY EVANGELISM

For decades, the evangelical church saw year-over-year growth. But today, the average local church across all denominational lines struggles to keep above sixty-five people in average worship attendance.[2] The fear that legacy churches would close faster than denominations or associations could plant new churches is no longer a fear but today's reality. Across the spectrum of Christendom, the church struggles to see more people in the pews than the previous year. Sure, outlier churches have seen increases in conversions and baptism, but the average church, regardless of region, struggles to find its footing in a shifting landscape of nones. So, what could

2. Earls, "Small Churches."

a church do when they find themselves struggling to attract new people to the church? Local members have to rely not on the pastor to win others to Christ but on each member using everyday evangelism tools to do their part in winning the lost to Christ and seeing the church grow.

Evangelism in the modern age is defined as spreading the gospel witness through preaching or public witness. Yet, in most churches, the pastor is expected to preach and share the message publicly while the congregation watches. Not every pastor or layperson is a Crawford; it will take dedicated lay leaders to see the church grow. So how? I'm glad you asked. It will take soft, intentional, and inspired evangelism to share about Jesus and to win people from the street to the pew.

Soft Evangelism

Soft evangelism is the most accessible form of sharing one's faith because it is nonthreatening and helps the member get comfortable with faith-sharing through a series of manageable steps. The big idea is to get a member comfortable with going out and witnessing and then take action to share their faith. Here are three easy and fun ways for church members to share their faith.

1. **Tip the Pizza Driver:** Have congregation members pray for the future pizza driver two weeks before the service. The goal is not to share pizza but to share the love of Christ through a generous tip. When the pizza delivery driver arrives, have them come forward, and ask what a typical tip for a single pizza is. When they share it, tip them generously, such as twenty dollars. Let the driver know you and the congregation have been praying not for a pizza but for the driver. The church had been trusting God would send the right person to the church. Ask if there are any prayer needs. Let the driver know that the congregation did not only want to pray for them but wanted to provide a larger tip. Put an offering plate or bucket out near the front of the platform and encourage

the congregation to come up and give. Have someone quickly count it, announce the count, and then celebrate with the driver how much they are loved and cared for by the church. Let the driver know if they do not have a church home, or are not working on a Sunday, you would love them to attend here. This is a simple but powerful reminder of Christ's love. I promise you they will be the church's biggest ambassador by sharing what God did through the church and how members blessed them.

2. **You've Been Ducked:** Rubber ducks have become the rage in many areas, especially with Jeepers, who own Jeeps. Other cars have taken up the ducking fad, with owners putting them inside the front windshield. This display got me thinking about what if the church attached a QR code or sticker listing the church website to a small portion of the duck. Provide these ducks to church members and encourage them to either give a duck to someone or leave it on a stranger's car when shopping, attached to a windshield wiper. It's an easy way to tell people about the church. Ducking should be done in a way that is not threatening to the one giving and the one receiving the gift.

3. **Logo Pen:** Several times a month, I find myself eating out and signing my bill with a pen that a waiter provides. It got me thinking: Why can't my church provide the pen that the waiter uses and then gift it to them? Every day, a handful of people ask the waiter for a pen to pay their bills at a local restaurant. What if your local church was the one who supplied the pens? Encourage your members to take pens from the pew back, or from a provided basket, with the church's limited information (name, website, mailing address, and phone number), and encourage members to gift the pens to the wait staff when they go out. Over time, the saturation of pens with your church's name on them will be everywhere in town. The goal is to share the church name with future guests and maybe even have them take that pen as a reminder of

a church they should check out. Like in corporate America, this tool is a subliminal message to share about the local church and Jesus through a nonadverse way of providing a need and maybe a little more.

Intentional Evangelism

Intentional evangelism is the act of planning, preparing, and promoting an event that will attract guests to the church property or inside the church. How often has your local church completed an event, and then a member asked why we did not get any new people to attend church? The mindset of one-and-done events has captured the local imagination and failed to render long-term results. Not everyone who comes to the church for an event is looking for a church home, but many are. With that in mind, begin to see these outreach events as opportunities to plant seeds in those who attend for a future harvest, not just opportunities to get someone in the pew the following week. People will come to events on the church campus who will be struggling with an issue, and your church can be a light of hope. The goal should not be to win them to the local church but to win them to Jesus. It starts by organizing a Christ-honoring event. Share Christlikeness in action by members, by creating opportunities to share Jesus. Then the church gets the honor of inviting them back to be a part of a Bible-believing church.

The outreach events at the church must not just be marketed for outreach. They should also have substance in sharing Jesus through actions and deeds. Be intentional in planning and implementing events that connect Christ with the community.

Inspired Evangelism

Inspired evangelism slows the growth mindset down so one can focus on obeying the spiritual call on church members' lives. Many in the church today did not come to Christ at a tender age but through a personal relationship or an acquaintance who shared with them the love of Christ as an adult. Regardless of the faith journey, members should be actively finding ways to share their faith stories with those around them.

Encourage members to begin each day by asking God for opportunities to share their stories with someone. Members will begin taking action with their faith by praying to cross paths with someone who needs encouragement, prayers, and a little Jesus in their day. What an opportunity to live out Christlikeness with your neighbors or total strangers. Allow happenstance to turn into holy opportunities to share the message of hope with others. It all starts with a simple prayer to bring someone along your path today with whom you can share. As you walk in a spirit of worship, allowing the Spirit to guide you, you will find more and more opportunities to share Jesus. Through transformational conversations, you will see God move in the words and the hearts of those involved in sharing and hearing Christ.

Everyday evangelism is about using church members' faith to infuse the world with Jesus while connecting to neighbors and strangers through daily activities. Through soft, intentional, and inspired evangelism, call your people in the church to win someone to Jesus by being a local evangelist for the church and God.

As Crawford won more people Jesus, the church began to grow. That led to the church having another problem. How to get the children and families to church. Crawford's husband was a fruit dealer and owned several flatbed trucks that he used to transfer fruit from the field to the produce stand. With the flatbed truck, the first bus ministry of the church was born. Each Saturday night the flatbed truck would have everything removed. Old fruit crates, tipped over, formed the primitive seating areas for children and families, and God began to move.

If your church finds itself struggling to gain traction after years of decline, there is only one hope: win a new person to Christ. Through persistence in sharing your faith, someone will come to know Christ through your lived experience. But, let's be honest, it most likely has been a long time since anyone has been led to Christ through your ministry or your personal interactions. Why? If you are a typical Christ follower, you lack a comfort level in sharing your faith with strangers. Faith sharing is challenging in a post-Christian America. In a 2022 study initiated by Lifeway Research and reported on by the *Christian Post,*

> the survey found that 54% of participants said they are either "willing" or "eager" when asked what they think about "telling others about Jesus Christ." However, 52% of Americans who identify as Christian believe that encouraging someone to change their religious beliefs is "offensive and disrespectful," and 66% of Christians are not familiar with any "methods for telling others about Jesus." Sixty-eight percent of respondents believe that "it is the responsibility of the pastor to equip the congregation to share the Gospel" and 69% agree that it's "the responsibility of Christians to encourage non-Christians to trust Christ as their savior."[3]

So, while our hearts may be willing, our mind and mouth do not connect in sharing our faith.

SHARING JESUS IN UNSTRUCTURED WAYS

I love Sundays. Each Sunday, I get the joy of attending church. Yes, I know I am the pastor, and some would say I "have to attend," but I love attending church. Sundays are when fellowship takes place with believers and those seeking a deeper walk with the Lord. You have probably experienced this too; you walk through the lobby and hear the conversations, see the warm smiles and friendly hellos, and overall you experience an atmosphere that welcomes others. Sundays are prime time for resharing about how Jesus has helped you during the week to reach others with the gospel.

As Sunday school starts, people begin to enter their spiritual silos that reflect their class, noticing still others linger in the lobby over a cup of coffee and continue their conversation; we began to rethink this time of in-between (between Sunday school and the

---

3. VanDyke, "Two-Thirds."

start of traditional church). A pastor asked a series of questions: Could Jesus still be here over coffee and conversation? Could Jesus be shared through coffee and conversation? The simple answer is yes. For many, Sunday school counts for the most spiritual among us, but what stops God from challenging us over coffee and conversation? Nothing.

My children's and families pastor came up with the idea of turning these unstructured times of conversation in our coffee area into sharing Jesus by steering the conversation toward how Jesus has impacted their lives in the last week. This unstructured Sunday school class enables the ebb and flow of people coming in and out of the conversation without realizing they are in a class. Hosting a class that is not a class has reminded me that Jesus works in different ways. Here are the lessons learned observing people get their coffee.

Lesson 1: Create a Space for Open Conversation

When the coffee area was created, it started as a connectional space that brought people together. Over time, the relationship aspect did not happen the way the leadership thought, and we took a hard look to remake the space with the resources we had at the time. That meant taking the coffee area from grab-and-go to adding an assortment of breakfast items, to create a space that encouraged people to slow down. With a set of hodgepodge furniture, the space began to feel different. No longer were people taking their coffee and running, but they began to sit down and have conversations that would begin to bring people together.

After several weeks of observing what was happening, several saw this as a real success. People enjoying their morning pastry at a table or lingering longer in the area. We planned to highlight the relational aspect of connecting over coffee with new furniture that draws people together. In a world that is so fast paced, slowing the pace down and enjoying the presence of the Lord through fellowship with believers can be a rewarding part of Sunday mornings. As people became more accustomed to sitting down, not pulling out their smartphones, they began to enjoy real conversation, which led to life changes and new friendships.

Lesson 2: Create a Space for Discussion

Polarization has not only affected the world but also seeped into the church. The church should be a haven for ideas and thoughts brought forth with a design to ask, What does Scripture say about this? In these safe places where no lead teacher or pastor is directing the conversation, the Coffee House has someone with strong faith to help direct and steer toward God-honoring responses. In these safe places, the conversation can open itself up to opportunities to share about one's faith, work concerns, and how God is and can help them through the season they are facing.

The coffee area has become a great mentoring tool for spiritual maturity and for growing spiritual individuals to learn from one another. The informal coffee class has brought ideas and ways to celebrate God through even the most challenging conversations. With this type of mentoring, we have seen less gossiping and cliquish behavior in the lobby, which has helped us grow more unified as a church. While it is not one large group but multiple smaller groups connecting in conversation, it still provides a sense of larger gathering in smaller spaces. As the leadership observed the area and overheard conversations, it was clear people had begun to develop more trust with one another, and a connective spirit had developed in the process.

Lesson 3: Create a Space for All

If you serve in the average church, you will notice an imbalance of one age group. The mark of a healthy church is an intergenerational fellowship where people of all ages, from the cradle to the grave, serve together to expand the kingdom.

Most churches already struggling with providing intergenerational connections have unintentionally created silos by collecting people together in age groups. This hinders creating a family atmosphere inside the church. The coffee area was designed to bring people together through conversation. I have witnessed that all age groups have slowed down to enjoy the space. We intentionally added children's snacks and juice boxes that are low enough that children can get the items themselves. For adults, we have provided expanded offerings outside of just traditional coffee and tea. These selections of fresh fruit, donuts, and other items have made the coffee area a must-go place to stop when a person enters the church.

As we expanded our breakfast selection, we encouraged children, families, and older members to sit, talk, and enjoy each other's company. Observing, you can hear the little conversations about Jesus and life change during the week. This is a win for intergenerational ministry and for ministry that is unstructured and guided by God. The Coffee House, as we call it, was reestablished with an eye toward future guests. We realized if we could create a welcoming place, develop a listening ear and an encouraging spirit, maybe the guests would want to stay and learn about God, not merely in word but indeed.

Across from the north entrance, looking out our lobby, is a six-story apartment complex built on the property we sold to the developer to pay off nearly seven decades of debt. For decades, the space was used for parking and had several buildings on it that housed our Sunday school department, church offices, and thrift store. But, with the sale, God brought us neighbors and helped us to get out of 1.2 million dollars' worth of debt that had become a significant burden on the church.

The Coffee House has become a gateway to meeting our neighbors, connecting with our community, and slowly evangelizing our neighbors over a cup of joe. You might not have a coffee area or neighbors, but God has given you ideas if you would slow down, pray, listen, and obey. As of this writing, I am unsure if it will become a full-blown coffee house due to city regulations, but I know this: if God wants us to move in that direction, we sure will.

Chapter 9

Believe Again: Dreaming Forward

THE SECOND SUMMER AT the church would continue to bring forth transformation. This time, the gym would become the epicenter of Believe Again, with a plan to turn the space into a community center. I say epicenter because it would cause another spiritual earthquake of change. The divisions would stoke passions on both sides, pitting ministry and mission against each other. For decades, the gym housed our Upwards basketball program, fellowship dinners, ladies' ministry, and weekly His Mission services, which provide spiritual and physical nourishment to primarily people experiencing homelessness in the city. To enact the plan, every ministry that used the gym would have to adapt. Several things had to happen to transform the space.

1. His Mission would need its own space.
2. The twenty-five-year-old gym floor would have to be replaced.
3. Black mold, inching its way down the rafters and walls, needed removal.
4. We would need buy-in from the congregations affected by the change or all the wins we had in the ensuing year would be lost.

The action of dreaming forward brought a new footprint to the campus. The summer of the Dreaming Forward fundraiser was not a spiritual nirvana—the hard conversations, emotional turmoil, and an overall sense that the wicked merry-go-round would never stop took hold for many. Even I was growing weary of all the side comments and just plan mean spirit that some folks had. Maybe it was from the loss of members, the negative words spewed at me by Christian brothers and sisters, or just the emotional toll change takes, but I was emotionally tired.

The focus on reconstituting a presence in the neighborhood would take more time and work. Did I have it in me? Could the church withstand more change? These and many other questions rushed through my head. The effort placed in this phase would challenge my leadership ability but also show God's plan repeatedly to even the most negative of bystanders. The fact of the matter was that God was not done with the church.

Redesigning the Footprint for the Future

The gym has hosted His Mission for nearly thirty years; it is an incredible ministry that provides a hot meal, worship service, and Sunday school on Sunday mornings and meals on Wednesdays. What I love about this ministry is that people care. The workers and volunteers poured themselves into this ministry. Ministry team members arrive at the church between five thirty and five forty-five in the morning each Sunday to prepare a hot meal for future guests. These unsung heroes labor weekly as the hands and feet of Jesus. They deserved their own space. For decades they had been vagabonds within the church culture. The church sits on 4.26 acres of land with two outbuildings and acres of land to the north of the property. Former duplexes that housed our Spanish church for decades were now open to be used. It was easy to see the connection between the ministry and this property. One of the two buildings was currently used as a thrift store, and the other would become the new sanctuary and kitchen for our Phase 2 Compassionate Ministry Center. While it might have seemed thrown together at the last minute to some in the church, it was part of longer-range plan that started nearly a year before.

In fact, six months before, the church board formed a compassionate ministry center that would house His Mission, the thrift store, and educational programs in two fifteen hundred square feet buildings a piece along with an acre of land, half of which was undeveloped. A church member had died the previous August and left the church a house in a residential neighborhood located in another city so that the proceeds of the sale could go to His Mission. With the sale of property, the ministry netted two hundred thousand dollars, which was put in a certificate of deposit (CD) until a plan was developed to use the capital funds. When looking strictly at His Mission, this would provide security for the ministry—having its own space, a source of income from the thrift store, opportunities for expansion using the empty lots next to the buildings, and cash to help offset building costs. If it were that simple, then you would not need a book or these final chapters. Nothing is simple in church revitalization. Even with the best laid plans, trouble still comes.

Relocating the Ministry

Within weeks of moving the ministry from the gym to the new campus buildings, members of the church heard over and over that the space was not "big enough." They were right. The original design was to knock out walls and reconfigure the footprint, but that advice was not heeded by staff who oversaw the ministry. The volunteers were used to a larger space in our church kitchen, and the smaller space kitchen area they found did not meet the cooking requirements. What the ministry needed was space for cooking and serving food. However, the push from staff and volunteers of the compassionate ministry center was to expand one of the two buildings not for His Mission but for the thrift store. What! I know, it does not even make sense writing about it now months later. The reality was the leaders needed reimagination of the current footprint of the buildings and property for current and future needs. Simply put, we needed imagination not consternation.

Looking back at this time, I squarely place the blame on myself for not leading better. Instead of leading from the front, I allowed other members and leaders to take charge. Some would say, "You empowered others." But in the end, as the undershepherd of the church, my role is to protect the flock. The question I asked myself: Was I really helping or hurting the local church? The situation was too divided and needed a strong leader, not a passive one. As the reader, you might disagree, but I have second-guessed my lack of full-throttle action time and time again. For some members, I did my best; for others, I meddled too much. It was a lose-lose situation because the temperament against change had become baked in within a small faction of the church. In the end the lack of clear and consistent leadership allowed a vacuum of voices to control the ministry, almost leading to a rebellion with the ministry completely collapsing or breaking away on its own. Thankfully, the corporate documents did not allow the ministry to break away from the church, and the church board (acting as the ministry board) held sway in the end through strong meaningful leadership.

COMMUNITY CENTER-FOCUSED

With His Mission relocated across the campus, the first step of the refurbishment of the gym was to deal with the black mold that some said was harmless but continued to grow down the rafters. Behind a wall that once housed a baptistry, it looked as if a fire had swept through the area because of the amount of black mold growing. Two years previous, the church had investigated eradicating mold but did not have funds and waited for another day. Honestly, I did not deal with the issue my first year, tending to other major changes that needed to take place, which led to another regret of mine. However, with a new year and a church budget designed to free up extra dollars that came from a slimmed-down staff, the time was right. Once the mold was remediated, we turned to painting the center. The color I chose would incidentally be the color the gym was decades before, according to a picture removed from the wall that hid the former color. Thus, we reached back into our history to celebrate the past while looking toward the future. In finding the same paint color as it had been before, the "coincidence" alerted the team we were on the right path.

Since that time, we've added an incredible new sports floor that matches our logo colors, creating a welcoming space for all. The floor allows us to host a variety of games, including basketball, pickleball, and volleyball. Our goal was to form four sports leagues, catering to children from kindergarten to sixth grade, with indoor basketball, street hockey, volleyball, and soccer. This would bring families to the church weekly outside of Sunday morning service, many of whom do not have a church home. We're also targeting senior citizens during the day with rec league–style games, such as pickleball, ensuring everyone feels included and valued—and it has worked! In renewing this space, we are seeing over two hundred different people using this space weekly.

We turned the lobby of this space into a gaming center that houses foosball, air hockey, a Pac-Man machine, video games, an eating area, and a coffee house. The space looks incredible and is reaching new families with children weekly through added programs such as cheerleading and Christian scouting. We invested in a part-time community center director and are redoing our central kitchen to prepare for the future. I have to tell you, these words do not adequately describe the transformation that has taken place in this space. Investing in this area has not come without a cost of dollars and people. Tens of thousands of dollars have been poured into this space to provide a safe environment for the community. The cost of building out the space is worth it if a child or person comes to know the Lord. For me and the church, they see it as a community connection point that could potentially be rewarded with future pew growth. What drives many of us is having the opportunity to share Jesus with someone who does not have a relationship with him today. Incredibly, we did this without going into debt. God provided the funds each step of the way through the generosity of God's people. I can't explain it except to say, when you obey God, he provides the resources for his plan.

CHANGING MINISTRY MEANS ADAPTING THE PLAN

In 2015 the church birthed a thrift store ministry that became a mainstay in the community. The thrift store ministry was dramatically changed when the church sold its property next door and forced the store to relocate elsewhere on the church property. For most of its years, it was a profitable ministry that provided resources to those in need. However, two months before I arrived as pastor, they began losing income. For the next fifteen months, they continued that trend. At first the income was blamed on the move from one side of the property to another, due to a lack of visibility from the street. Even though it moved less than half a city block, some in the community could not find the new location. Whatever the reason, the store was declining. Faithful volunteers poured themselves into saving the store, but the ledger remained negative month after month. Board members suggested the store change its hours, add more days the store would be open, and expand merchandise. Volunteers and employees pushed back, stating the store was breaking even or that they had tried the remedies suggested before. The reality was that the ministry, designed to be the economic engine of His Mission, was borrowing monthly from savings to keep afloat. Even when I drew on a large dry erase board in the office conference room the given data from their own financial reports, some connected to the store suggested they were false numbers. In researching thrift stores in the area, we found eighteen within city limits and thirty-six within a thirty minute drive of our current store. The community did not need more thrift stores, but they did need a community-focused church.

The former thrift store board, made up of volunteers and mostly former church members, was dissolved, and the church board became the new board. The church board took a more active role in the ministry and began trying to right the sinking ship. For months, the board reviewed financial documents, monitored the monthly sales, and held critical meetings with the directors of the thrift store and His Mission. These consequential meetings led to the thrift store's dissolution and His Mission's expansion into the thrift store space. In the end, the reality was too stark. The board had to act. The board adapted to the new reality and leaned into food insecurity as the focus of the compassionate ministry center, and transitioned out of retail ministry.

WHEN A MINISTRY CLOSES

Let me share with you what I learned in closing a ministry. In any revitalization setting, leadership must constantly evaluate the works of the church and how it impacts the community. From time to time, these evaluation periods will lead to the evolution of a ministry by either adapting to new circumstances or closing the program altogether. Months of evaluation, long conversations with stakeholders, and an eye to where the community would be five years from now was what drove our shift in ministry strategy. Ministry is not about keeping open a ministry for ministry's sake but serving the current and future needs of the community. Sometimes that means letting go of something loved to see the value in the next season of ministry in the church's life.

Share Compassion with All Who Are Affected

When an announcement of change is made, raw emotions bubble to the surface that can be seen through the varied actions of those impacted by the change. Change is not easy; it becomes painful when it affects an area that a person has poured themselves into. As a leader, you must allow emotions, good or bad, to be shared. Allow compassionate directness to take place when you share why a decision was brought about, allowing for complete transparency. After the announcement of the closing ministry, there was a vicious backlash from a small group of passionate members and nonmembers who supported keeping the ministry open. Telephone calls, emails, and personal visits voiced their displeasure at the closing.

A passionate (non-church member) advocate volunteer in the closing ministry visited me in the office. She gave me a passage of Scripture on love that her pastor had written in the church's worship folder. I thanked her and promised to read it, but I was working on a funeral message and would review it later. She then handed me a little plastic Jesus, and I again thanked her. As she turned away, she turned back and said, "Because you need Jesus! As you do not have the love of Jesus in your heart." Then she turned and walked out. In a moment of shock, I said, "Well, praise God," in the voice of Eeyore from Winnie the Pooh. Sometimes ministry is like this lady who shared her emotions through guerilla warfare, where she came in to shame me. She had a right to share her feelings even if I did not like how she said it to me. Let me encourage you to allow God to guide you as you move forward by sharing compassion even when you do not want to. The actions of each person speak to where they are in Christ, not where you stand. Compassion is not a dictation but a lifestyle of heart holiness. When someone gets angry, you move to peace. Give permission to their grief. Allow grief to be shared, but also share the truth of why the ministry had to close and the next steps that will follow.

Spirit-Led Decisions Will Not Free You from the Demands or the Disgruntled

Major decisions should not be made flippantly. Think about it this way: data-driven decision-making reviews raw data, not emotions or people that a decision may affect. Take the emotion out of decision-making, and focus on what the numbers say about whether the ministry is effective. When the decision is made, it must be shared clearly and transparently. Explain how the decision was brought forth. I shared discussion points, financial data, numerical data, and the process of what happened in a board room with those who earnestly sought the answer to "why did this happen?"

While not sharing names, I share voting outcomes and the thought processes of those in the room in real-time as best I remember them. Why? Because church members deserve transparency in leadership and practices. However, even being transparent does not persuade everyone from their thoughts and feelings about the process. As a leader, you will have to choose to be led either by the spirit or by self. Sometimes that means allowing the negative to come and ignoring the gossip. While it might be hard, your role is to heal the church, not keep dividing it by arguing one side or the other.

Stand as a peacemaker in Christ. Explain fifty times the same reasons to those who ask. It will show that you are spirit led, will not back down, and will continue to pray that healing can come. It is not easy to weather assaults from church members, but in leadership sometimes it is lonely at the top. In my own situation even as the verbal assaults came, some began withholding their tithes as a punishment to me, or even left the church. I trusted God. Let me challenge you to trust that if the Lord leads you to a decision, he will lead you through the decision-making process.

Serve with Excellence Until the End

If you have to transition a ministry, there is a temptation to give up because the ministry will close anyway. But the reality is that you are called not to serve a ministry but the Lord. The Lord has called you to finish the race to the end, not give up because things did not work out as you had hoped. As you lead your people through a disappointment, focus not on the closing but on serving in new ways through the Lord. God has an incredible plan for the local church, but its people are giving up too easily, disappointed by life, and failing to live out their calling. I cannot urge you enough to dig down deep and focus on the main thing, the Lord, and not give up when things do not go your way.

As the end draws near, what an opportunity to remember what God has done through the ministry. Spend some time reflecting on the past while projecting a bright future for the church.

Believe Again: Dreaming Forward

Ministry is ever changing. Closing one ministry and opening another has been a fluid cycle of the church for centuries. Do not take it personally, but rely on a personal relationship with Jesus, who will guide the church to the next thing he wants the church to focus on. While we faced an ending, we also saw just on the horizon a new beginning, and well, that is exciting. Remember this: God's plans for the local church or even a person's ministry are far more than a program but are a partnership with Him and the surrounding community.

Chapter 10

The End Was Just the Beginning

DURING THIS SEASON OF dreaming forward, I saw the church become a community-focused, Christ-centric ministry trying to reach the community. The thrift store closed, and His Mission's footprint has expanded into the store's old space. The reality is that ministry is never done. It is constantly changing and adapting to the current and future realities that the neighborhood faces. Any thriving ministry must maintain Christ at the center and adjust its spirit to move where he leads. The leaders of the compassionate ministry center stepped down and left the church, which enabled us to realign the direction of the ministry even further. As the church grieved another loss in the leadership ranks, I saw an opportunity amid discouragement. In my spirit I knew God was ready to provide a new vision for the compassionate ministry property.

Evaluation Leads to Evolution

The church board focused intently on reimagining the compassionate ministry center. In the old showroom of the thrift store, the church board, acting as the Phase 2 Compassionate Ministry Board, sat and began discussing what was next for the ministry.

The store had closed, the leaders had stepped down, but instead of seeing it as a negative, they began to dream again. If you find yourself in a downward situation, you can either continue to spiral out of control or dream again. It is in the dreaming that God begins to move in your favor. For some members, it had been years since they had stepped foot on that portion of the property. What they saw shocked and appalled many. The center dedicated to helping others needed help. Instead of voicing negative dread, the board chose to speak life into the ministry. Through conversation, prayer, and investment of funds, they became determined to turn around this ministry. When facing a downcast situation, all stakeholders must be willing to take inventory of what really is taking place. The ministry space was no longer conducive to the ministry standards we had set for ourselves elsewhere on the property through the year of Believe Again. If you are pastor, you must help lead your board to the next step, but they must make it if it's going to take root and grow. I had done my part; now they had to step up and act. The reality was that ministry could not go on the way it was. It was either going to thrive or die. Simple as that.

As the board evaluated the needs, they began to see what could be done with the space. Within an hour, they voted to update the kitchen, add new flooring, paint the walls, fix holes and exposed wires, overhaul the electrical work in one of the two buildings, add new signage with new logo, develop a community garden, and name new codirectors focusing on ministry and mission. How did they do this? They had been good stewards of their resources. A year prior, the church board had accepted and then sold a piece of property with the funds invested in a CD with a brokerage house. There were a host of issues they could have spent it on, but instead, as part of the long-range plan, we invested those dollars. The board's decision over a year before enabled them to act by reinvesting dollars into a space that would restore lives. Do not skip over that lesson. Sometimes God provides resources not for today but for tomorrow. As a leader you must help your people see that saving, investing, planning, and acting are not an overnight sensation but a spiritual lifestyle that uses godly principles to turn around a local church.

Developing a Clear Mission with a Ministry Focus

The mission of the ministry became crystal clear to the leaders, supporters of the compassionate ministry center. For the first time in decades, the leadership was beginning to work from the same plan. The turnaround began with clear direction and focus on the ministry's mission. If you want to thrive and not just limp along in ministry, you must learn from your mistakes, evaluate the past, look toward the future, and always focus on serving as Christ. If I am honest, where we lost our way was a lack of directional oversight from the pastor and church board. We failed in providing clear parameters for staff and volunteers and then enforcing those parameters when they were stretched. The lesson learned during the summer of Dreaming Forward provided opportunities to grow past our mistakes and to lean more on God. Hopefully, you will learn from our mistakes and grow as we did.

It Is Never Too Late to Admit Mistakes and Learn from Them

The leadership team admitted through their series of votes to redesign the ministry that we had failed. While I did not vote, I failed in proper oversight. I take full responsibility, and that is why I stand committed to righting the spiritual ship. As leaders there is a tendency to not want to admit mistakes. That is a mistake, a big one in my book. Mistakes are part of life, and they are valuable lessons. Be willing to admit mistakes. Learn from the mistakes, and then make them right. Today the ministry is a shining example of perseverance. In the end, we are a church in progress. The cyclical nature of church revitalization is that the church's work is never completed. God has called each lay member and leader to help build the church. As a legacy church, we prayed, believed, and sought God's will to reach our neighbors with the gospel each day. The work is hard and sometimes downright painful.

Are you ready to take the next step to help your church rise from the ashes into church renewal? Are you ready to stand and fight for God's vision for your local church with an open mind and heart, and trust God? If yes, get ready, buckle up, and watch how God will guide your local church.

Epilogue

When God's Call Became My Yes

As they say, I have written the book on church revitalization—seven books, counting this one, and hundreds of articles and podcasts on the subject. Personally, this church has challenged me more than any other. The year before I arrived at WHNaz, the Lord worked on my heart. God was calling me to say yes to another assignment, and I was fighting to stay at the current one. Over the previous year, nine district superintendents, including one who visited me in my community from several states away, asked if I would be willing to relocate and help lead a struggling church back to health. God was trying to get my attention, but I was unwilling to say yes. I had not sent out any resumes, yet God was laying my name on the hearts of district leaders. If you are outside my denomination, subtract the words "district superintendent" and add the word "state executive" or "state overseer." You will understand the magnitude of what God was doing.

    Several leaders hosted me through Zoom and connected me with an open church, but I turned down the offer to move forward each time. The reality was that God wanted my yes, and I was stuck at no. In early winter of 2022, the Florida District leader reached out. There was no doubt in my mind it was another attempt by God to get my attention. This time, I allowed the God process to play out further. The conversation with the district leader was kind

Epilogue: When God's Call Became My Yes

but direct, as I had no intention of leaving my assignment. I was pastoring a fantastic church in eastern Kentucky. The church was a vibrant, growing church; my family loved the people and the area. The idea of leaving the church and relocating a thousand miles away to Florida had no attraction to me. I had grown up in Florida and had zero desire to move back. Yet, God was moving me closer to a yes.

Five months before the fateful phone call with the Florida District superintendent, a hurricane had delayed our vacation to visit our family two and a half hours south of Winter Haven. We rescheduled the vacation for the spring of 2023. In speaking to the district leader, I was three weeks away from returning to Florida, and he asked if I would visit the church during my vacation. I agreed to a candidate weekend. In my mind, I said yes to an interview in order to help the church board think through what church revitalization would look like in their context. Typically, on these candidate weekends, the candidate's spouse would attend the board interview, the candidate would preach, the church board would host a meet and greet with the candidate and congregation after the service, and sometimes provide a meal.

As I did not intend to become the church's pastor, I wanted to provide a blunt assessment on what I saw and heard that weekend. In setting expectations, I shared that my wife would not attend the interview but would attend the Sunday service, that my seven-year-old son would not participate in the interview weekend, and that I was not sure I would even say yes. I was inching somewhat grudgingly in the direction of a yes. The interview with the church board was heartfelt and honest. Each member of the board was forthright in sharing the church's perceived problems, and it was clear they desired a leader of action and change. After a six-and-a-half-hour visit, I traveled back to where I was staying. God gave me a lot to think and pray about. That night, my yes got a little closer to God's.

By the end of the candidate weekend, the church board would vote unanimously to call me, but I was not ready to commit my yes. In my system, calling a pastor would be a several-step process.

Epilogue: When God's Call Became My Yes

Step 1: The church board had to vote overwhelmingly for the candidate.

Step 2: The candidate had to agree to have their name presented to the church.

Step 3: The church board secretary would announce the upcoming vote twice during formal worship services.

Step 4: The pastoral candidate would need at least two-thirds of the votes cast by members present on the day of the full congregation's vote.

My candidacy was delayed for a month as it fell around Easter, and during that time, a couple inside the church lobbied members of the church and church board to vote against me. I would not find this out until much later. After a four-week waiting period, election day came, and with all the ballots counted, I received a 76.6 percent call to be the next pastor. It was the worst call of my ministry. As I had never received anything under 90 percent, I was now further from a yes. If I were advising a revitalization candidate in the same situation, I would have said, Run! Do not go to that church. But God was drawing me, maybe pulling me closer to a yes. Even as I delayed my answer to the district leader by three days, God used the space and time to get me to a yes. In those three unsettling days, the Holy Spirit was drawing me in. I could not fathom leaving a safe place that I loved and taking on a church where nearly 25 percent of the church did not want me. However, after three prayerful days, God called me to a new place, and I had to say yes.

The story shared in these pages has been a story of God's redeeming power not only in the local church but also in me. God used the revitalization of the local church through the Believe Again campaign. The revitalization effort restored faith in his people and drew me closer to him. In reality, church revitalization is challenging but rewarding when a church submits to God's plan and follows through. I pray you have found hope, inspiration, forthrightness, and a renewed commitment to your calling in these pages because God is calling you to submit your yes to him.

Other Books by the Author

Helping the Small Church Win Guests: Preparing to Increase Attendance

Confidence for Leadership: Influencing with Skill and Integrity (coauthor)

Missional Reset: Capturing the Heart for Local Missions in the Established Church (coauthor)

Revitalize to Plant: Reshaping the Established Church to Plant Churches (coauthor)

Addition Through Subtraction: Revitalizing the Established Church

Revitalizing the Declining Church: From Death's Door to Community Growth

Bibliography

Barrett, Desmond. *Addition Through Subtraction: Revitalizing the Established Church.* Eugene, OR: Wipf & Stock, 2022.

Bauman, Virgina Lohmann. "Beyond the Legacy Church Building." *The Christian Citizen*, Oct. 20, 2023. https://christiancitizen.us/beyond-the-legacy-church-building/.

Betzer, Dan. *Why Some Churches Are Blessed: Putting Faith and Obedience into Action.* Springfield, MO: Gospel, 2015.

Burge, Ryan. "My Church Is Closing, and I Don't Know What Comes Next—For Me, or America." *MSN*, July 25, 2024. https://www.msn.com/en-us/news/us/my-church-is-closing-and-i-don-t-know-what-comes-next-for-me-or-america/ar-BB1qEbKk.

Carpenter, Tim. "Kansas Universities Demolishing Old Buildings to Save Millions on Deferred Maintenance." *Kansas Reflector*, Dec. 28, 2023. https://kansasreflector.com/2023/12/28/kansas-universities-demolishing-old-buildings-to-save-millions-on-deferred-maintenance/.

Chandler, Diana. "Mark Clifton Brings Vitality to Rural America Church Landscape." *Church Leaders*, July 8, 2022. https://churchleaders.com/news/428916-mark-clifton-brings-vitality-to-rural-america-church-landscape-bp.html.

Cheyney, Tom, and Steve Sells. *Life After Death: A Strategy to Bring New Life to a Dead Church.* Orlando, FL: Renovate, 2019.

Church of the Nazarene. "GA2013: Dr. Gunter's Morning Devotional." Aug. 22, 2014. Video, 22:38. https://www.youtube.com/watch?v=JB8N-NdaVck.

Crosby, Fanny. "Redeemed, How I Love to Proclaim It." In *Praise and Worship: The Nazarene Hymnal*, 247. Kansas City, MO: Nazarene, 1951.

Earls, Aaron. "Small Churches Continue Growing—But in Number, Not Size." *Lifeway Research*, Aug. 21, 2024. https://research.lifeway.com/2021/10/20/small-churches-continue-growing-but-in-number-not-size/.

———. "Southern Baptists Lost More Than 1,200 Congregations in 2022." *Lifeway Research*, Apr. 2, 2024. https://research.lifeway.com/2024/04/02/southern-baptists-lost-more-than-1200-congregations-in-2022/.

Evans, Elizabeth E. "As Episcopal and Other Mainline Denominations Face Clergy Shortage, Creative Workarounds Are Redefining Ministry."

Bibliography

Episcopal News Service, July 31, 2023. https://www.episcopalnewsservice.org/2023/07/31/as-episcopal-and-other-mainline-denominations-face-clergy-shortage-creative-workarounds-are-redefining-ministry/.

Hartford Institute for Religion Research. *Back to Normal? The Mixed Messages of Congregational Recovery Coming Out of the Pandemic.* Aug. 2023. https://static1.squarespace.com/static/64f9c635272a564e247f1f4c/t/65a54b64265f9c5510a13e7c/1705331561743/Epic-4-2.pdf.

Huffington, Arianna. "Microsteps: The Big Idea That's Too Small to Fail." *Thrive Global*, Nov. 5, 2021. https://community.thriveglobal.com/microsteps-big-idea-too-small-to-fail-healthy-habits-willpower/.

Nadeem, Reem. "Many Americans Like Online Religious Services but In-Person Still Preferred." *Pew Research Center's Religion and Public Life Project*, June 2, 2023. www.pewresearch.org/religion/2023/06/02/online-religious-services-appeal-to-many-americans-but-going-in-person-remains-more-popular.

Nazarene News Staff. "General Secretary Releases 2023 Statistics." *Church of the Nazarene*, Jan. 25, 2024. https://nazarene.org/article/general-secretary-releases-2023-statistics.

Neuman, Scott. "The Faithful See Both Crisis and Opportunity as Churches Close Across the Country." *NPR*, May 17, 2023. https://www.npr.org/2023/05/17/1175452002/church-closings-religious-affiliation.

OnSolve. "One Call Now: How It Works." One Call Now, Jan. 10, 2024. www.onsolve.com/platform-products/critical-communications/one-call-now/how-it-works.

Rosen, Ellen. "As Hundreds of Churches Sit Empty, Some Become Hotels and Restaurants." *New York Times*, Aug. 6, 2024. https://www.nytimes.com/2024/08/04/business/church-development-reuse.html.

VanDyke, Nicole. "Two-Thirds of American Christians Don't Know Any Methods for Telling Others About Jesus, Poll Finds." *Christian Post*, June 2, 2022. https://www.christianpost.com/news/two-thirds-of-christians-dont-know-methods-for-sharing-jesus.html.

Winter Haven Board. "Charles Kirby Celebration." Unpublished report, Winter Haven First Church of the Nazarene, Winter Haven, FL, Feb. 1988.

www.ingramcontent.com/pod-product-compliance
Lightning Source LLC
Chambersburg PA
CBHW071442160426
43195CB00013B/2000